# GOLDEN WALK

*Foreword by Global Pastor Tommy Barnett*

# GOLDEN WALK

*Following Wisdom Into Heaven*

## RUBEN GONZALES
### XULON PRESS

Xulon Press
2301 Lucien Way #415
Maitland, FL 32751
407.339.4217
www.xulonpress.com

Unless otherwise indicated, Scripture quotations taken from the Holy Bible, New International Version (NIV). Copyright © 1973, 1978, 1984, 2011 by Biblica, Inc.™. Used by permission. All rights reserved.

Paperback ISBN-13: 978-1-6628-3152-2
Hardcover ISBN-13: 978-1-6628-3255-0
Ebook ISBN-13: 978-1-6628-3153-9

# TABLE OF CONTENTS

Once in a good while comes to us a book that we simply cannot put down when we start to read it. I remember the slogan "Inquiring minds want to know"; well, who doesn't have an inquiring mind, especially when it comes to the subject of heaven. No matter where you have been to on this great planet of ours, heaven defies every conceivable thought we might have of its beauty.

Every question you could possibly have about heaven has an answer in this book as Ruben helps you navigate through it all. My questions that I hadn't even thought about asking are covered, and of course the trend of "wisdom" in this, his third, book follows right along the same path.

Remember, we are talking about eternity here. This means that we will have all the time in the...I was going to say "world," all the time, period, to talk to the saints of old; our relatives and friends will all have a story of how they got there.

Follow along page after page as heaven is brought to you in full color and in 3D, 4D, I don't know, surely many dimensions. One thing is for sure, you will never be so glad that you accepted Jesus than after you finish reading this book. If you have never asked Jesus in your heart, you will certainly want to as He not only gives us an awesome life here but he also offers a great retirement plan that is "out of this world."

Joel Perales
Pastor, Evangelist
www.peralesministries.com

Golden Walk: Following Wisdom into Heaven, is the third book of award winning Christian author Ruben Gonzales' series on Walking in Wisdom.

A hallmark of Mr. Gonzales's style is telling engaging stories interwoven with timely, powerful scriptures and spiritual truths and this book follows richly in that fashion.

As the third book in a series of three, this book is set into three parts: Get Ready, Get Set, and Let's Go. These sections lead the reader through receiving salvation through Jesus Christ, what comes next after salvation, and finally, what Heaven is really like. (Hint: we're not going to be resting on clouds.) It's more beautiful and glorious than we've ever imagined.

Mr. Gonzales is a gifted storyteller and wordsmith, and you will enjoy his engaging vignettes of family life. He draws readers into his stories in such a way that you feel like you are part of his family. But he doesn't write to receive acclaim for himself. He writes to tell as many people as he can how to receive Jesus as Lord and Savior and enter into a life that will be eternal.

Is Heaven a question for you or for a loved one? This book will give you sound, Biblical answers. Our unpredictable times are the evidence of the groans and labor pangs of creation Romans 8:22 speaks of. Time is growing shorter and circumstances are becoming more desperate for people who do not know the truth of Jesus Christ.

This book is a gift to yourself, to loved ones, friends and neighbors. Don't hesitate. Buy it for yourself and gift a copy to a loved one while you're at it. It is a fountain of hope and truth in a world gone mad.

Shelly Morales,
Aglow International;
English teacher; photographer

# ACKNOWLEDGMENTS

**My Heavenly Father** – You have always been there for me no matter how many times I have failed You. Soli Deo Gloria!

**The Lamb of God** – I will follow You into Heaven.

**Holy Spirit** – Thanks for your comfort and inspiration!

**Irma** – Without your love, support, and encouragement, no one would be reading this.

**Mary and Ramon Gonzales** – You always provided in abundance all that you had.

**Family and Friends** – Whether related by blood or love, thank you for loving me in the good and the bad. There are way too many to name without offending someone by unintentional omission.

**Pastors, teachers, authors, worship leaders** – your influence continues to form me and increase my faith.

# FOREWORD

## by Tommy Barnett

Global Pastor, Dream City Church, Phoenix
Co-Pastor and Founder, LA Dream Center
Author, *What If*

I t is all for the Glory of God alone that I wholeheartedly endorsed the first two Christian books, *Barrio Walk: Stepping into Wisdom* and *Broken Walk: Searching for Wisdom*, written by Ruben Gonzales. This book, *Golden Walk: Following Wisdom into Heaven*, completes what Ruben calls the **Walking in Wisdom Series**. God has had His Hand on him as the three books have been published in the past three consecutive years. Mr. Gonzales has found a need and is filling it through his writing. He fully understands that many raised like him are not privileged to hear the entire Gospel. He wants others to see the full Bread of Life scriptures he did not receive until mid-life.

As Children of the King, we must do all we can to help each other on this earthly walk as we follow Jesus into Heaven, *"Blessed are those who have learned to acclaim You, who walk in the light of your presence, Lord"* (Ps. 89:15). I am so proud of Ruben as he has demonstrated his conviction to share the Good News. He uses a blend of life experiences, humor, and well-placed scriptures throughout his books. We share a mutual love for our Lord knowing He is the One that keeps our steps steady and sure.

His main purpose for writing *Golden Walk* is to provide others with scriptures and biblical stories that were not disclosed to him until age 47. His father did not accept Christ as Lord until age 78, about two months before his death. For the remainder of his life, Ruben vows to tell everyone he can about how Jesus Christ changed his life. There are many lessons in *Golden Walk*; you'll enjoy reading "No Blueberries in the Barrio."

*Golden Walk: Following Wisdom into Heaven* is divided into three parts. Part one, "Get Ready," will help people understand how it is imperative to receive salvation. It includes teachings on forgiveness and repentance. The second part, "Get Set," talks about what to do after receiving salvation; this includes, reading the Bible, witnessing, and baptism. The third part, "Let's Go," gives insight on what we can expect when we reach Heaven. The reader is offered hope and excitement about our transition into eternity. This book provides a roadmap built on *Golden Steps* to encourage readers and increase faith.

Mr. Gonzales grew up in the barrios of Phoenix, Arizona, and East Los Angeles. He spent two years in a seminary in Compton, California. He is a Vietnam veteran who struggled with alcohol for 30 years. Although he had success while working 39 years at the US Postal Service, he has experienced the darkness of being separated from the Truth. Ruben also cherishes the joy that comes from accepting Christ and having a new song placed in his heart. He understands the purpose for the remainder of his life is to do God's work by the writing and speaking of His Goodness — everything we do is all for the Glory of God alone.

*"May the God of Hope fill you with all Joy and Peace as you trust in Him"* (Rom. 15:13). Until we meet in Heaven, find a need and fill it. I love you!

# INTRODUCTION

## GOLDEN WALK: FOLLOWING WISDOM INTO HEAVEN

I t is with complete faith in His promise that I know I will walk before the Lord in the Land of the Living. He has saved me from being entangled in the darkness of death. I was smothered by the anguish of the grave. Even though I was overcome with confusion and distress, I managed to call upon the name of the Lord. He heard me and I will call on Him for the rest of my days until my soul returns to His Rest.

He delivered me from death, he dried all the tears in my eyes and reset my balance, so I am able follow Him into Eternal Life. *Golden Walk* is about sharing the Wisdom I have learned on my crooked path of life. Walk with me, grab Wisdom by the hand, and get a glimpse of Heaven. Each journey begins with a single step. Get on this path and follow the golden brick road. May each page you turn pull back the curtain so you can see His salvation. He is the only Way to get back Home to the Father. Immerse yourself in the Living Waters of His Word, and Wisdom will enter your heart and Knowledge will refresh your soul.

My prayer is *Golden Walk* is like sunscreen with a strong sun protection factor (SPF). After all, I do not want you to get burned, and it can get mighty hot down there. You will have to apply scripture on you for protection and then make sure you are covered when you are exposed to the burning rays of sin. SPF is also the acronym for reduced **S**tress, improved **P**eace, and increased **F**aith; it has the SPF rating of 3:16. This is the best sun protection plan for rain or shine.

Everybody wants to go to Heaven, but no one wants to die. To get to Heaven, we must live for what is eternal by dying to self. Sounds like a lot of rhetoric, huh? *Golden Walk* is about choosing to live for what ultimately matters. My prayer is your personal relationship with Jesus is intensified. He is the only Way; the unseen title for this book is really *Golden Walk: Following* Jesus *into Heaven*.

Every breath we take on earth is a blessing, every day another page in the book of your earthly life. Live each day so your last chapter has a great ending. That way when you wake up on the other side, you take the first step of your Golden Walk on the Street of Gold. Get ready! Get set! Let's go!

# PART ONE – GET READY

# CHAPTER 1

*"Teach us to <u>number our days</u> that we may gain a heart of wisdom"* (Ps. 90:12)

When I meditated on the above scripture and prayed for a heart of wisdom, the little voice asked me to begin counting. As soon as I got to one, I heard the inaudible word, "STOP!" I stopped and pondered on the number one. The revelation hit me like a lightning bolt. If I take care of one, (the only day I am guaranteed), everything else will fall in place. It's so simple, yet profound—count to *one* and take it one day at a time! Count to one and make the changes you need to make in yourself before you go trying to change everybody else. Numbering our days begins and stops with the number one.

Take one step in the right direction by making one choice (Jesus). Follow Him one day at a time. He is the One Way (Jesus) for us to reach our one eternal life...enjoy the journey with me as we go on this *Golden Walk*. Let Him take your hand because He will not let go; if we take His hand, we might let go when the going gets rough.

## One Creator = God...One Race = Human...One Problem = Sin...One Solution = Jesus

*"For there is One God and One Mediator between God and man, the man Christ Jesus"* (1 Tim. 2:5).

If you knew someone you love were dying, would you treat them differently? Would you overlook the disagreement that caused distance in your relationship? If so, fix that relationship *now*. We have no way of knowing when our last day on earth will be, so now is the time to live *today*, as if it is your last day. Show kindness, get rid of the poison of unforgiveness, and share what you have, as you cannot take it with you.

## Make It Day One instead of One Day

If you keep saying, "I will do it one day," you may never see that day. Instead of saying, "One day I will do it," say, "Day one of when I took my first step to make the needed change." Pray like this: *God, give me the serenity to accept the things I cannot change – and the wisdom to know when the one that needs to change is me.*

Yesterday, I was filling out a survey that wanted to know my age. It had several groups of number ranges such as 46–55 and 56–65. Mine was in the last category; it was marked at 66+. I laughed and told my wife, Irma, "I'm in the 'next!' category at the front of the line to croak." You see, I am now in the plus category at an old but healthy 68. I keep getting advertisements for funeral arrangements. How rude! One of them even said, *"Buy now,* before the *cost of living* price increase." I'm looking forward to finally get rid of this annoying ringing in my ears (tinnitus) that will soon turn into *singing* in my ears.

4

Any way, it won't be long now before I get to see those 12 gates, each gate made of one single pearl and walk the street of gold. I love imagining about the following scripture: *"The twelve gates were twelve pearls, each gate made of a <u>single pearl</u>. The great <u>street</u> of the city was of pure gold, like transparent glass"* (Rev. 21:21). Can you envision the size of an oyster that can produce a pearl large enough to make a heavenly gate? And one street of gold as pure as transparent glass? It won't be long now before I get to see Jesus, and there will be no more sorrow. Jesus will be my everlasting light, and the sun will never set again. I will rejoice in the bounty of the Lord and eat from the Tree of Life that awaits us in Heaven.

The Tree of Life that was in the Garden of Eden, *". . . bearing twelve crops of fruit, yielding its fruit every month. And the leaves of the tree are for the healing of the nations"* (Rev. 22:2). It brings joyful tears to my eyes just thinking about the things that God has prepared for those who love Him. If our eyes are the windows to our soul, then maybe, our tears provide the extra ingredient we need to get a glimpse of heaven. *It won't be long now!*

By the way, those of you that hang around me will eventually hear this corny saying of mine: "It won't be long now; that's what the monkey said when he got his tail chopped off by the lawn mower!"

## Grains of Sand

*"How precious to me are Your Thoughts, God! How vast is the sum of them! Were I to count them, they would outnumber the grains of sand ..."* (Ps. 139:17-18).

Did you know that God can use a grain of sand to humble you? A few years ago, after I received recognition at work, I was strutting like a rooster in front of my place of employment. I looked down and saw an ant rambling across the sidewalk. A thought entered my head when I saw it. I am to this ant like God is to me, and I could kill it right now. As I decided the ant's fate, that inner voice from within my soul said, "Compared to Me, you are like a grain of sand at the bottom of the Indian Ocean." Wow! What a humbling revelation! I immediately asked God to forgive me for having such a vainglorious attitude.

Earlier this year, while at the beach, God used grains of sand to humble the driver of a new vehicle equipped with lots of bells and whistles. The truck had everything but toilet paper. What do you call a new truck without four-wheel drive on soft sand? Answer: Quatro Cinco!—all four tires submerged in countless grains of sand. If the driver had read his vehicle manual, he would have learned that his new vehicle was equipped with traction control. With one push of the button, the driver could have spared himself of humiliation, frustration, and anger by taking the traction control off. Guess who the driver of the new truck was.

We go through life with our personal traction control set to on. We think we can speed through the sand dunes of life without any fear of getting stuck. Life becomes easier when we set our personal traction control to off and let Jesus take the wheel. Hmm! I bet you can almost hear Carrie Underwood singing right now. I also hear the lyrics, "On Christ, the Solid Rock, I will stand; all other ground is sinking sand."

How many grains of sand are in an hourglass? Who knows? Who cares? How many grains of sand are in your "hourglass" that represents the length of your life? I certainly care about that as I know my days are numbered. Time is running out for all of us. My job in retirement is to write about our Heavenly Father (Three in One) so I can help others on this Golden Walk as we march toward Heaven.

Think of *Golden Walk* as a blueprint of what we need to do to win the race called life. Using the Apostle's words in **2 Timothy 4:7** we must finish our race like Paul. *"I have finished the race, I have kept the faith. Now there is in store for me the crown of righteousness."* The first part of this book is to get you ready by increasing your faith. Each scripture that is referenced is a building block made of spiritual gold. Let His words be a lamp to our feet as we follow wisdom (Jesus) into Heaven.

Here is a thought that came recently from a revision of the Serenity Prayer.

> ***God, Grant Me the Serenity to Accept People I Cannot Change***
> ***The Courage to Change the One I can***
> ***And the Wisdom to Know when the Change Needs to Be Me.***

From *Broken Walk: Searching for Wisdom*, "A young man tries to change the world … a wise man does better by changing himself."

If you want to accept Christ as your Savior and have Him take control of your life, say a prayer like the one below and sincerely ask Him to be your Savior:

*"Lord Jesus, I believe you are the Son of God. Thank you for dying on the cross for my sins. Please forgive my sins and give me the gift of eternal life. I ask you into my life and heart to be my Lord and Savior. I want to serve you always."*

Our days on earth are numbered, but our days in eternity are immeasurable like *grains of sand.*

## Time, Our Most Precious Resource

As paperboys, my two brothers and I cherished our time to sleep. We stayed in bed as long as we could but still manage to get the newspaper route completed on time. Delivering newspapers was challenging for a nine-year-old, especially the chore of waking up at 4:30 a.m. The desert mornings were dark and cold in Phoenix during the winter. Getting dressed became a wrestling match when putting on two pairs of pants and double sweatshirts with a jacket. We did not have gloves, so we wore socks on our hands. We would sleep as long as we could and then be in a spasmodic tizzy to get to the newspaper station.

We had a "paper punk" friend (that is what we called each other) named Johnny that would come to our back door to wake us up. Occasionally, we would coax Johnny into lying on the floor as we all enjoyed some extra sleep. After a few more zzz's, we would wake up abruptly and then blame Johnny for not waking us up. He would tell us, "I did wake you up, but you told me to lay down!" We would tell him he had to make sure we got up on time next time; this usually happened about twice a week.

The four of us would then rush out and make up time, by "taking the freeway" on our bicycles. Phoenix was relatively small in 1961, and the newly constructed Black Canyon Freeway was close to our house. We would ride our bicycles as fast as we could down the northbound entrance near Jefferson and then exit on Adams. Somehow by the grace of God we never got any speeding tickets.

Sometimes in life we make up time by rushing or taking risks. Perhaps we drive faster than we should as we figure out the exact time we can leave for work without being late. There are unforeseen circumstances along the way that may increase our risks. The more risks we take, the larger our chances of messing up. Perhaps the risks come in other areas like stretching a rubber band or blowing up a balloon to its breaking point. As we get older, the risks become different like how much quality do I really need to put into my product or service and still maintain maximum sales.

Another risk is knowing the checking account balance is lower than the check that was just written with the hope the deposit will clear on Monday. This happened to me as a young man discovering the convenience of credit cards. It also taught me a tough lesson on getting into the 'paying interest' trap. Whew, I'm glad those days are long gone.

*Time is our most valuable resource*; once it has passed, you will not get it back. Risks are the chances we take when trying to make up time. One day, Jesus will return, and only each of us, individually, can determine if we will be ready for His arrival. *"The bridegroom was a long time in coming, and they (ten virgins) all became drowsy and fell asleep"* (Matt. 25:5). Read this parable as it tells us of 5 wise virgins who were ready with enough oil for their lamps. There were also 5 foolish virgins who had to go out and buy oil. The foolish virgins lost time when buying oil and ended up losing their entrance into the wedding banquet as the door was shut. They asked the bridegroom to open the door. *"But he replied, Truly I tell you, I don't know you"* (Matt. 25:12). This story is for us now as there is still time to wake up. The day or the hour of His return is not known. "Wake up, paper punk!" Be ready with some oil (salvation) in your lamp.

When the trumpet call of God sounds in the rapture, those who are 'born again' will be taken up to meet the Lord in the air. You *do not* want to be left behind. Make sure you accept Jesus as Lord and Savior while there is still time. The rapture will happen in the twinkling of an eye. You will not have time to pray or repent. You're not going to have time to run to church and make things right. You won't be able to reach your favorite pastor for advice. Besides, any pastor left behind is not worth talking to.

## The Free Gift of Salvation

One of the first lessons I learned about salvation came via a short story written by my favorite author, Max Lucado. It has been close to 20 years since I read this vignette, so I am writing it to the best of my recollection. My recollection is somewhat hazy, but I want to share the gist of this story.[1]

Back in the early 1800s Napoleon Bonaparte was the emperor of France and led the French troops to victory in numerous battles. After one of these hard-fought victories, Napoleon rode his horse back to the French encampment. When he dismounted his horse, the stallion galloped away at a high speed. There was a private nearby that jumped on a horse and managed to chase Napoleon's horse and bring it back to the emperor. When the private handed the reins to Napoleon, he saluted the private and said, "Thank you, Captain!" The surprised private returned the salute and said, "Yes, Sir!"

The private, now captain by fiat, moved all his belongings to the officers' quarters. He received his new uniform and privileges without any questions because Napoleon said it, so just like that, he instantly became a captain. Napoleon made the private a captain just because he had said it was so.

*Here's my question, why can't we just accept the gift of salvation from God in this same manner?* We do not have to earn our salvation; Jesus paid for it with His death on the cross.

Becoming Christian is as easy as ABC as outlined in these Bible verses:

A. All have sinned and come short of the Glory of God (Rom. 3:23; 6:23; 1 Jn. 1:10).

B. Believe on the Lord Jesus Christ, and you will be saved (Acts 16:31; Jn. 1:12).

C. If you Confess with your mouth that Jesus is Lord and believe in your heart that God raised Him from the dead, you will be saved (Rom. 10:9; Eph. 2:8–9).

Don't be like that dude in charge named Felix found in the book of **Acts, Chapter 24**. Felix had the opportunity to listen and learn from Apostle Paul. Here is part of this story: "*He [Felix] sent for Paul and listened to him as he spoke about faith in Christ Jesus. As Paul discoursed on righteousness, self-control, and the judgement to come, Felix was afraid and said 'That's enough for now! You may leave. When I find it convenient, I will send for you'*" (Acts 24:24–25). Felix blew it, he missed his opportunity. Don't be a Felix; instead be like Paul. One day we will see Paul in Heaven, not sure if Felix will be there. There are many persons that have heard the message of salvation but are still non-committal — their time is running out. If you know any of them, just say, "What's up, Felix?" Then be ready to explain what you mean.

Where you will live for eternity can still be determined right now. The choice is yours, *today*, to have your name written in the Lamb's Book of Life.

Enjoy the ride for the remainder of your life. There will be some bumps along the way, so put your trust in the Lord so He can help you stay on the right path.

## It Begins with Unshakable Faith

"If I could only touch that garment!" The unnamed woman with an issue of blood felt cut off from God and by man. The doctors offered her no hope, but she knew that Jesus was in town. Due to his popularity for healing the sick, there was a large crowd around him. She believed wholeheartedly that if she could just touch the hem of His garment, she would be healed. When she reached out to Jesus in faith, she was instantly rewarded with a supernatural release of power from the Son of God into her life. What an awesome story as Jesus said to her, "*Daughter, your faith has healed you. Go in peace and be freed from your suffering*" (Mk. 5:34).

If you are going to join me in following Jesus into heaven, it begins with unshakable faith. If you need comfort from your suffering, reach out and touch the hem of His garment. This isn't just for physical healing, it includes any challenge you may be facing, for instance, finances, addiction, or broken relationship. It begins by establishing a personal relationship with Him. When you have taken your last breath on Earth, it is just you and Him. Confession to man will not be your ticket to get inside the Gates of Heaven. No act of generosity, compassion, or service will get you in. It is belief and having unshakable faith that God sent His Son Jesus from Heaven.

You must believe that Jesus paid it all for us by giving up His life for us on Calvary. You must come to know He is the *only* way to the Father. He proved it by resurrecting from the dead and ascending into Heaven. He is seated at the right hand of the Father waiting for us with arms reaching for us. Jesus is in that same position as He died, with His Arms open wide. His life poured out of Him from the injuries He suffered. He did it willingly for us, He took the scourging, the falls under the weight of the cross, the insults, the spit, the crown of thorns, the nails, and the spear to His side. The glory of Christ, the image of God, was on full display that day. Now we must let His Light shine out of our hearts so others can see God's glory of the gift He gave us: His only begotten Son. *"All this is for your benefit so that the grace that is reaching more and more people may cause thanksgiving to overflow to the glory of God"* (2 Cor. 4:15).

When Jesus was nailed and raised on the cross, it was the final triumph as He continues to draw all people to Him. Without the shedding of blood there is no forgiveness of sin. We must develop unshakable faith and stand firm until the end—no matter what we face. Then we can take that *Golden Walk* into paradise and praise Him for eternity.

## An Awakening of Faith

*"As long as the earth endures, seedtime and harvest, cold and heat, summer and winter, day and night will never cease"* (Gen. 8:22).

My seedtime came the moment I raised my right hand, asking Jesus to reign in my heart. This seedtime minute arrived when I finally understood the entrance of Your words into my ears. *"Consequently, faith comes from hearing the message, and the message is heard through the word about Christ"* (Rom. 10:17).

My breakthrough moment came on November 13, 1999, at Primera Baptist Church. It came after hearing a powerful message that convinced me to ask Jesus into my heart. I was awakened from a spiritual 'dirt nap' (slang for death) as the pastor's words entered my ears and galloped into my brain. My brain was like a dry sponge that expanded when the Living Water saturated it. As my brain capacity was enlarged, my forehead wrinkled and seemed to tug on my eyebrows opening my eyes wider so I could take in more Sonlight. My seedtime

13

came as my right hand went up past the spiritual grave to get me out of the smothering darkness.

It was a miracle of transformation that happened instantly like the changing of water into wine or Lazarus being called out of the grave. It was awesome to get that taste of death out of my mouth and to wipe the mud off my eyes. Better yet, my soul proclaimed: "It is finished" as I was transformed into a New Creation. *"The entrance of Your words give light; it gives understanding to the simple"* (Ps. 119:130).

There was a sweet aroma that surrounded me that special day. I was like a seedling that had just sprouted into the light coming out from a parched, thirsty desert. The smell of the desert after some much-needed reign (rain) is incredible. It is hard to describe the scent of God, but here is my best attempt. *"The scent is like the voice of the desert praising with a parched sound that sends an aroma of gratitude to our Creator."* My favorite smell in the entire world got better as my exposure to the Sonlight (Word of God) gave me increased strength. The scriptures were like the canals of Phoenix I swam in as a young man. Then, at age 47, the words from the Bible flowed like living water to nourish the root system of my heart. I am thankful because your verses kept my eyes wide awake through the night watches (my dark times of alcohol, gambling, anger, and more). My favorite verse soon became John 15:5: *"I am the vine, you are the branches. He who abides in Me, and I in him, bears much fruit; for without Me you can do nothing."* I have continued to grow as I abide in the Sonlight for the Glory of God alone.

It is a blessing to have spent the past 21 years in the harvest of my new life. It is awesome to be able to rise before the dawning of the morning and ask for wisdom. The Bible says: *"If any of you lacks wisdom, you should ask God, who gives generously to all without finding fault, and it will be given to you"* (Jm. 1:5). Just two days ago, I meditated on the word "begotten".

You know, the word used in John 3:16: "For God so loved the world that He gave His only *begotten* Son that whoever believes in Him will not perish but have eternal life." To man, the word "begotten," as defined in Webster's dictionary, means something created. To me, in my spiritual understanding, the word "begotten" now means "not created." The spiritual meaning of begotten is "always was and always will be." I support my definition with this scripture, *"In the beginning was the Word (Jesus) and the Word was with God, and the Word was God"* (Jn. 1:1). So my question to Mr. Webster is, "How can begotten mean something created when the Son of God always was and always will be?"

As believers, we know that God created us. This basic understanding is the foundation of our faith. God is to be praised as the Creator, known by His marvelous order and beauty of His works. He has power to redeem, recreate, and renew even those buried tightly in the darkness of the world. Our dependence on God is really a moment-by-moment existence that calls us to live lives of devotion and gratitude toward Him. We need to push ourselves through the grave and into His Light. It is our purpose to help harvest others into Heaven. It is our Seedtime and Harvest. Join me in calling out to Jesus. *"Everyone who calls on the Name of the Lord will be saved"* (Rom. 10:13).

My prayer is this book will convince or reinforce your belief that Jesus is the *only* way to the Father. I believe one day there will be persons I have not met talking to me in Heaven about how they came to know the Lord. My hope is that you are one of them; then our joy will be complete. Stand firm in faith and be courageous and strong as you tell others about Him; speak the Truth in the spirit of Love as our *days are numbered* and we will soon see His Glory.

Start counting, and when you get to *one,* stop. There is only *one* God, and there is only *one* way to get to Him. What is that way? Find the answer in John 14:6.

**Golden Step #1: Make it day one rather than one day.**

# CHAPTER 2

*"And so we know and rely on the love God has for us. God is love. Whoever lives in love lives in God, and God in them"* (1 Jn. 4:16).

The frog does not worry about where his next fly will come from. Have you ever seen a sparrow leaving its nest with a lunch bucket under his wing? The bee instinctively knows it will find pollen when it leaves the hive. *If they do not worry, why should we?* The flower does not worry about the seasons. The moon shines bright even with no power of its own. God knows what we need before we even ask for anything. We are carried in His Love, no matter what tomorrow brings. Remember to **f**ully **r**ely **o**n **G**od (F.R.O.G.) like they do, every day, every moment. Here's something to smile about: Can you imagine the surprise the former tadpole (now turned frog) received when he zapped his first insect with his long tongue?

Did you know a hippopotamus does not have go to the store to buy sun protection lotion? That's because God included in their metabolism the ability to produce their own sun guard.[2]

Here's some God-given features custom-made just for the hippopotamus. Hippos spend most of their day resting in the water and can hold their breath for up to 30 minutes. They have sensitive skin, and the areas where they live can really get hot. God made the hippo in such a way that they make their own sunscreen via a secretion that looks like *pink* sweat. Hippos have no true sweat glands like we do, but their pores secrete a pink layer of mucus to prevent sunburn. How about that — the hippo doesn't need to waddle over to Walmart to buy sun protection lotion. *"Let everything that has breath praise the Lord!"* (Ps. 150:6). The pony is the only animal I know that has difficulty praising God because it is a little hoarse (smile).

**Trust God** — worrying carries tomorrow's workload using today's strength. It does not empty tomorrow's burdens; it just empties the strength we have today. When we worry, it is like paying rent for a place that we may never see or live in. Relax, God is in control, He will provide — make it a practice to thank Him in advance! Thanking in advance is part of our faith that really pleases God.

We must become childlike and relearn how to dance in the rain instead of being upset at the storm. We must praise even when we are hurting the most in our darkest hour. Especially in those faith-testing moments when we cannot comprehend why something so horrible or unfair just happened. Remember, even if we fall seven times, we must rise again. Dust yourself off, stand firm in faith, be courageous and strong, speak the Truth in Love, and get ready to see His Glory. My hope is you are given the spirit of wisdom and revelation so that you may come to know the Lord Jesus Christ even better.

One of the areas I still need help with is patience, and Lord, I need it *right now*! Here's a coping skill I have developed on how to deal with red lights when I'm driving behind schedule. The moment comes when I'm approaching a red light. My thoughts go to: *Will I make this light? At what point do I continue through the intersection if the light changes to yellow? Do I speed up? Are there any police officers around? Cameras?* I have learned to remind myself to take a breath and know I will get there when I get there. If the light doesn't change and I proceed uninterrupted through the intersection, I *give praise*. If I am stalled at the intersection by a red light, I *give praise*. Either way, *God is going to be praised*! We can't control when the light is going to make us come to a stop, but we can control how we react to it.

## My Father's Jump into Heaven

My greatest blessing in life came at the moment of my father's death. That was more than 19 years ago. It changed my outlook on life and reset my vision to always look up for the answer. I used to look at life as if searching for solutions to life's problems through a microscope. My life got much better when I started seeking God as if looking up through a telescope and trusting Him for the answer. *"Trust in the Lord with all your heart, and lean not on your own understanding, acknowledge Him in all you do and He will make your path straight"* (Prov. 3:5-6). It worked for me as I stopped being wise in my own eyes and learned to fear (be in awe of) the Lord and shun evil.

Grab a glass of milk, maybe a couple of cookies, and enjoy this short story that I hope increases your faith as much as it has mine. This is a story that is stuck on continuous loop in my brain, and I will not stop telling others about it—all for the glory of God alone.

God took care of my father as he was slowly dying but did not know it. His health and strength were dwindling away slowly out of his body like a drip from an IV plastic bag. About two months before his passing away, I took a week off from work in McAllen, Texas, to spend time with Dad in Phoenix, Arizona. I took my father to see his cardiologist, and the doctor told him, "There is nothing I can do for you, but at least you won't have to make another appointment with me." It was an awful feeling driving him home with a lump in my throat that served as a dam to stop my emotions from gushing out. My father arrived home in good spirits and proudly announced to my mother, "See? I told you there was nothing wrong with me. The doctor told me I did not need to make another appointment."

Right then, I realized my father had no clue that his life was almost over. I chuckle when I think about one of his favorite questions to me over the last few years of his life. He would ask me, "Do you think I'm gonna make it, man?" I also remember on several occasions during my life, my father would talk about how shameful it would be if he were drunk when the Lord came back. He said it in Spanish, "*Qué feo sería si El Señor regresa y me encuentra aquí borracho.*" This means, "How awful if would be if Jesus returned, and I were drunk." He worked so hard all his life in the fields, he served in the Army during World War II, spent 30 years or more working at the City of Phoenix, and then worked another 10 years at USPS as the best custodian in USPS history.

A couple of days after that doctor visit, my mother and sister had some errands to run, so it became my turn to stay with him. He was getting weaker by the day and spent most of his time in bed. I walked into his room confidently armed with my Bible in hand and spirit filled with the prayers from my church family in McAllen. My heart was heavy as I saw my frail "Papa Joe" in bed, too tired to get up. When I went into his room, he said he could not understand how he could not get out of bed. He told me, "If only I could eat a little bit, I know I would feel better." He looked through his bedroom window at his citrus trees and forcefully said, "Look at my lemon trees, I need to get out there and pull the grass that is growing around them." At that precise moment, two birds hopped joyfully onto the windowsill. I told him, "Dad, look at those two birds, they don't worry about anything!" He growled at me and snapped, "What are you talking about, man?" I remained calm and said, "Let me show you."

I opened my Bible to Luke 12:24–26 and softly read, *"Consider the ravens: they do not sow or reap, they have no store-room or barn; yet God feeds them. And how much more valuable you are than those birds! Who of you by worrying can add a single hour to your life? Since you cannot do this very little thing, why do you worry about the rest?"* He looked at me and said, "I didn't know that was in there."

I asked him if he wanted me to show him more, and he nodded yes, so I quickly flipped the pages of my Bible to John 14:1–6. I explained to him this happened way back before the Last Supper. I told him Jesus was saying goodbye to His disciples as He knew he was about to be crucified. *"Jesus said, 'Do not let your hearts be troubled. You believe in God; believe also in me. My Father's house has many rooms; if that were not so, would I have told you that I am going there to prepare a place for you? And if I go and prepare a place for you, I will come back and take you to be with me that you also may be where I am. You know the way to the place where I am going.' Thomas said to him, 'Lord, we don't know where you are going, so how can we know the way?' Jesus answered, 'I am the way the truth and the life. No one comes to the Father except through me.'"*

My 78-year-old father looked surprised and said, "I didn't know that was in there." I asked him if he wanted me to show him more. It made me feel good to hear him say yes and then watching him as he sat up a little higher like a child being read a bedtime story. The Bible does say that to get to heaven we must have child-like faith. My fingers were in hyper speed rushing to the book of Romans 10: 9–10, 13. I boldly read to him, *"If you declare with your mouth, 'Jesus is Lord,' and believe in your heart that God raised him from the dead, you will be saved. For it is with your heart that you believe and are justified, and it is with your mouth that you profess your faith and are saved...for, 'Everyone who calls on the name of the Lord will be saved.'"* At this point, my father's eyes were brighter and more focused. I asked him, "You believe Jesus is Lord, right? And you believe that God raised him from the dead, right?" He replied yes to both questions, so I continued by asking him if he wanted to hear more, and he firmly said, "Sure!"

We moved to the last chapter, Revelation 3:20, and the words seemed to jump off the page of my Bible and ran right into his ears as I read: *"Here I am! I stand at the door and knock. If anyone hears my voice and opens the door, I will come in and eat with that person, and they with me."* I paused and told my father Jesus was knocking on the door of his heart. I touched his chest and knocked gently near his heart. I asked him if he wanted to invite Jesus into his heart as his Lord and Savior, and he said yes. I wanted to do a somersault right then, but instead, we bowed our heads, and he repeated a simple prayer asking for forgiveness, acknowledging Jesus as Lord, and thanking God for raising Jesus and us from the dead.

When I looked up at my father, he had a goofy smile on his face. For the first time I could ever remember, he even looked kind of nerdy. He asked me, "Do you think I'll make it, man?" I smiled and replied, "You already have." God had just worked *another miracle*, one of the greatest blessings I had ever received. We hugged each other as I tucked the blankets of God security around him. As I left his bedroom, my heart was swollen and almost bursting from joy. He slept peacefully that afternoon, and my mother asked me whether I had given him something to help him sleep. I responded that I had not. Little did she know that he had received a healthy dose of the gos-pill (gospel).

As I was getting ready to leave back to Texas after a couple of days, I put my forehead on my father's forehead and looked deeply into his misty eyes. *If the eyes are the window to our soul, then maybe our tears serve as that extra ingredient to be able to peek into Heaven.* I told him, "If I don't see you again, I'll see you up there!" as we both pointed up. I *fully rely on God* to accomplish our reunion in Heaven soon.

My father continued to slowly fade away physically over the next few weeks. His voice became weaker, and I had to squeeze my ears to hear the juice of his voice. His last words to me were, "You're a good son!" and after I hung up the phone, I cried. I somehow knew these were the last words I would hear from him.

On March 14, 2002, I was busy at my job as the postmaster in McAllen, Texas, when I received a phone call from my sister Anita. She told me dad only had 24–48 hours to live, and he had slipped into a coma. I dropped everything and hurried home to pack up the Riviera. Irma, Anthony, and I left for the 20-hour drive from McAllen to Phoenix at 1:00 p.m. The drive was difficult, and I thank God that Anthony (around 16 years old at that time) helped me when I needed it most at about 2:00 a.m. Irma struggled to keep us both awake as she would sometimes fall asleep in the middle of her singing. We reached Tucson around 8:00 a.m.; I thought daylight would make it easier to drive, but the Arizona sunlight burned instant sting into my bloodshot eyes. The drive was physically and emotionally draining for the three of us.

It was stressful because I wanted to sleep like Rip Van Winkle while at the same time needing to beat the clock of death.

We arrived at my parents' house shortly after 9:00 a.m. My family was surprised when we walked in undetected through the open garage. My father looked skinny and was in a coma-like sleep. It made me feel good when he smiled after he heard my voice. We all stayed by his bedside most of the day and talked with him. I knew he could still hear me, so I was able to express my love for him. I even forgave him for the time he had me pull the sparkplug wire off the faulty lawnmower while it was still running. That was one of my first lessons in the school of hard knocks he gave me as a young boy. Irma and I sang songs to him throughout the day. He loved to hear us sing "Silent Night" during our Christmas visits. At the end of the song, he would clap and then asked us to sing it in Spanish, and we would.

During that day, I remember my brother Ernie, who has Down Syndrome, stand at the doorway of my father's bedroom with his arms crossed. He looked sternly at my father and said, "Hey, close your mouth, you're gonna catch flies!" He then said, "I'm not gonna worry about him, I got my own life to live." I felt badly for Big Ern because he was coping as best as he could. Little did I know that next morning after dad had died, I would hear a commotion outside. It would be from Ernie crying while furiously punching the plastic recycle bin. I would have to comfort him and bring him back inside.

As my father's life was about to end, at about 9:15 p.m., my sister Anita, who had been his primary caretaker, announced to my father that she was leaving. She told him she would be back to see him in the morning. At that moment, my father began to struggle for breath. We (mom, Anita, Ernie, and I) rushed to his bedside. My sister said, "It's okay, Daddy, the angels are all around you." She even rang the small bells of the angel wind chimes that were dangling above his bed. The bells sounded like a tiny choir of angels delicately singing.

Then *another miracle* happened. I leaned in close to my father and said, "Dad, jump into Jesus's arms!" My father, who had been flat on his back all day in a coma-like state, sat up and reached out—he took three last gasps, and he was gone. He then dropped back onto the bed as his soul left the room. It was the most beautiful, surreal moment of my life. There was so much peace and tranquility at that moment that is beyond my understanding. It was the closest I have ever been to Jesus as my father reached out to Him.

I stayed in the room as I wept holding the back of my father's head in my right hand. It surprised me to feel joy and gratefulness overflowing and saturating my body. My father had finished the race. Even though he was absent in his body, he was now present with the Lord. I went outside and talked to my siblings about it. We sniffed my right hand as our father's smell was still on it even though he was already in Heaven. *"Precious in His eyes are the death of His saints"* (Ps. 116:15). All Glory to God!

Remarkable! It happened just like Jesus said, *"No one comes to the Father except through me."* Jesus took my father to Heaven, and that day God showed me my father's salvation. My Tio Joe (now rejoicing in Paradise) was overjoyed to see my father's salvation through my words when I described to him what happened during my father's last moments. Are you ready to see God's glory through your own salvation? How about for your family? It is time to accept Christ—because the Kingdom of God is near.

The scripture also says, *"Believe in the Lord Jesus, and you will be saved—you and your household* (Acts 16:31 NIV). It's simple, all we must do is believe and *fully rely on God.*

Nothing speaks more clearly than God's Love as the Cross. Jesus said, *"And I, when I am lifted from this earth, will draw all people to myself"* (Jn. 12:32). He knew the kind of death He would die but did it anyway. *If Jesus can die for me, the least I can do is live for Him* and help draw all people to Him. *"This is how we know what love is: Jesus Christ laid down his life for us. And we ought to lay down our lives for our brothers and sisters"* (1 Jn 3:16). We have to be *all in* for Him as He was *all in* for us. We might one day be slain because of our faith. *Will you be able to stand firm and refuse the mark? Will you be able to keep the faith if you are being incarcerated because of it?*

When Moses was trapped between the Red Sea and the Egyptians, he told the Israelites: "Do not be afraid. Stand firm and you will see the deliverance the Lord will bring today!" (Ex. 14:13). Our God never changes; He is still a Way Maker and Miracle Worker. He will clear our path for us to reach the Promised Land if we remain faithful.

When you become a follower of Christ, you have passed from death to life and are filled with His Love. Anyone who does not love remains in death. My best advice: *if you want to take the first golden step* on that Street of God, you must first visit the Cross and believe in the name of His Son, Jesus Christ. We must *fully rely on God* and demonstrate it by loving one another as He has commanded us. Being *all in* takes full repentance, total obedience, and complete forgiveness of yourself and others.

Statistics show that one out of one persons die. When we are absent from the body, we are present with the Lord, if we have been born again in Christ. So here's a thought on the other side of death and where a sinner will spend eternity. When a sinner is absent from the body at death, is their soul immediately in the clutches of Satan? I don't have that answer, and my prayer is none of us personally find out.

No one goes to Heaven or Hell by accident, they go there because of a deliberate choice. That choice is to accept Jesus or deny Him. Jesus said it clearly in Jn.14:6 – He is the only way to the Father.

## Forgiveness

I cannot stress enough the golden brick made from the ingredient of forgiveness. You must forgive and forget. *A heart that is planted in forgiveness does not dwell on the past.* I once talked to a friend that told me anytime he got into a fight with his wife, she becomes historical. I asked him if he meant hysterical. He said, "No, *historical* — she always brings up my past even though she said she had already forgiven me for this." It would be a terrible fate if God became historical toward us. The Bible says, "... *as far as the east is from the west, so far has he [God] removed our transgressions from us*" (Ps. 103:12).

Examine your heart and ask God to shine light in it to detect if there are any specks of unforgiveness in there. The remarkable thing about forgiving someone (especially when it is the last thing you want to do) is it sets the prisoner free. The prisoner is not the person who did you wrong, the prisoner is you. Sometimes your offender has no clue you are holding a grudge. The poison of unforgiveness hardens your heart and takes away life flow with thoughts of revenge or other forms wishing evil on your offender, such as voodoo, curses, and slandering.

Whoever that person is, make time to forgive them sincerely and move on with your life more freely. It is good for your heart like eating Applejacks cereal. If you are old enough you might remember the slogan and song "A bowl a day keeps the bullies away." You can see that in this case the bully is *unforgiveness*, and it can stop you from getting to Heaven.

Let me explain: we will be forgiven as we forgive. It is part of the Lord's prayer. *"For if you forgive other people when they sin against you, your Heavenly Father will also forgive you"* (Matt. 6:14). It would be eternally catastrophic to be denied Heaven because of unresolved issues with someone who offended you. Even if you don't speak to the offender, have a conversation with God, and ask Him to remove the venom from your thoughts and heart — *as far as the east is from the west.*

**Golden Step #2: A heart planted in forgiveness does not dwell in the past.**

# CHAPTER 3

## WALK IN OBEDIENCE

*"Blessed are all who fear the Lord, who <u>walk in obedience</u> to Him"* (Ps. 128:1)

Adam and Eve had it made; they were full of freedom and walked around the Garden of Eden full of life, unafraid of anything. *"Adam and his wife were both naked, and they felt no shame"* (Gen. 2:25). All they had to do was follow God's first command, which included a reference to death. It says in Genesis 2:16–17, *"You are free to eat from any tree in the garden, but you must not eat from the tree of the knowledge of good and evil, for when you eat from it you will certainly die."* Notice how God states, "When you eat" in this verse. God knows us better than we know ourselves and makes known what is best for us. He loves us so much; He gives us the freedom of choice. We must do our part by trusting Him and continuously *walk in obedience*.

Unfortunately, when they disobeyed God, they died spiritually instantly and would eventually die physically. Death happened right away as the act of disobedience poisoned their souls. Their physical being still functioned as blood still flowed through their bodies, but now their special connection to our Creator was destroyed. Adam and Eve then hid from God as His presence brought on panic rather than peace. When God called them, *"They hid from the Lord God among the trees of the garden. But the Lord God called to the man, 'Where are you?' He [Adam] answered, 'I heard you in the garden and I was afraid because I was naked, so I hid"* (Gen. 3:8–10).

Adam and Eve hid and attempted to cover themselves with fig leaves they had made for coverings. It was not enough, and the intimacy with God came to a screeching halt. The guilty couple was kicked out of the Garden of Eden. All of us have been born outside of the Garden ever since, but there is Good News ahead near the end of this chapter.

My youngest grandson, Samuel, at four years old sometimes struggles with being obedient. In a recent conversation after he received his parole from timeout, he explained his predicament. He told me, "I want to be good and try to be good, but then something inside of me happens, and I get in trouble." This sure sounds like something Paul, formerly known as Saul, wrote in Romans 7:15, *"I do not understand what I do. For what I want to do I do not do, but what I hate I do."* Our problem is we are born with a heart problem brought on from original sin. Although we want to do good, evil is inherently right there with us. Samuel is an awesome boy with boundless energy. He is a young daredevil who does not consider the consequences when swinging too high or jumping off the sofa while trying to touch the moving ceiling fan. He is improving, and during our latest two-day visit, he managed to stay out of timeout and did not get 'panked. He has trouble saying the letter "s" on some words.

My brother Big Ern has Down Syndrome and can do no wrong—except when he cannot resist midnight snacks.

When he and Mom visited us in Texas a few years ago, we tried to devise ways to keep him from the pantry. We loosened light bulbs so the lamp would not work, placed chairs for barriers, and made him promise every night not to sneak food into the bedroom. On one of those nights, Irma heard a noise and saw the light on in the pantry. When she turned the light off, she heard some bumping noises inside the pantry. She thought, "Surely not," so she opened the door and caught Ernie raiding the pantry. We found empty potato chip bags, candy wrappers, and cookie crumbs in various places throughout his bedroom after they went home.

Ernie has a special place in my heart. Lately he has become somewhat serious and recently asked me, "Come on, Luben," (can't say his r's) "tell me the truth; is there really a Heaven?" What would you tell him? I shared the story from John chapter 14 when Jesus was saying goodbye to his disciples. Afterward He said the Sinner's Prayer with me and left the room smiling.

Below is a simple copy of the Sinner's Prayer just in case you missed it in Chapter 1. It is meaningless if the words are not sincere. We cannot earn salvation; we are saved by God's grace when we have faith in His Son, Jesus Christ. All you must do is admit you are a sinner, believe that Christ died for your sins, and ask for His forgiveness. *Have you done that?* What matters most to God is the attitude in your heart and your honesty. Man will always look at the outward appearance, but God looks at the motives in our heart. May I suggest praying the following prayer to accept Christ as your Savior:

*Dear God, I know that I'm a sinner, and I ask for your forgiveness. I believe Jesus Christ is Your Son. I believe that He died for my sin and that You raised Him to life. I want to trust Him as my*

*Savior and follow Him as Lord, from this day forward. Guide my life and help me to do your will. I pray this in the Name of Jesus. Amen*

Remember, we are not perfect, so we will continue to sin. We do, however, serve a perfect God, who is merciful and will clean us up with the verse I call "The Christian Bar of Soap." *"If we confess our sins, He is faithful and just to forgive us our sins and cleanse us from all unrighteousness"* (1 Jn. 1:9).

Early on in my childhood, my curiosity always seemed to keep me locked up in trouble. At that point in my young life, I was not quite five years old and spent a lot of my time entertaining my younger three-year-old sister named Lupe. She was lanky and not comfortable walking on uneven surfaces. Her manner of walking outdoors looked like a newborn colt taking its first steps, sort of like Bambi on ice. We did not get to spend much time outside without adult presence. One of my favorite things to do was to show off for "Lupeanuts," the nickname I gave her. (Today, Lupe is so sweet as a grandma, her nickname could now be "Lupeaches.")

On this particular day, I decided to demonstrate to her how the rooster walks. As we slowly walked down our neighbors' dilapidated sidewalk, we were careful not to step on any of the plants they were growing. There was a damp and musky smell because our neighbors grew whatever they could wherever there was dirt. They had *hierba buena* (mint), cilantro, jalapeños, and tomatoes. I told Lupe to stay back as I stretched my legs and struggled to straddle over the small fence quickly so I would not be seen by my mother. Like most kids at that age, I was sneaky and quick—a bad combination.

When I saw the rooster strutting on the other side of the fence, I went into a conceited stroll of my own. My head bobbed while I stretched my imaginary wings and raked the ground with my feet. My sister laughed as she enjoyed my rooster imitation act. I felt like I was about to sprout feathers and could hardly wait for the next sunrise. My selfie could have been posted on a box of Kellogg's cornflakes.

Much later in life I learned, "There are three things that are stately in their stride,....*a lion, mighty among beasts, who retreats before nothing; a strutting rooster, and a he-goat*" (Prov. 30:30–31 NIV).

All of the sudden, I looked up and was staring eye-to-eye with a rooster that did not like being mocked. He had a look in his eyes that said, "Oh heck no!" I made a futile attempt to intimidate the cock by giving him my fiercest mean-mug look. It did not work as the stupid rooster went into attack mode. It scared me into running faster than my little legs could go and I fell to the ground. I thought to myself, "This is going to hurt." To this day, I'm not sure if I fell on my own or the rooster gave me a flying double kick. That no-good yard bird proceeded to do a tap dance on my back and pecked on me like a large corn on the cob. I screamed while the rooster bit and scratched me for what seemed like an eternity (probably less than half a minute).

Our neighbor, Chavela, heard the commotion and ran out of her house with her broom swinging. She yelled, "*Gallo condenado, te voy a matar!*" That means, "You sorry rooster, I am going to kill you!" Chavela was animated and always wore a bandana like Rosie the Riveter. She spoke in a rapid-fire vocabulary that mixed choppy English with Spanish. She picked me up and rushed me into our house. Chavela apologized profusely, and I remember my mother saying, "It's his own fault; I told him to stay away from the rooster."

They laid me on the bed and brought out the *sangre de chango* (monkey's blood), also known as iodine, to put on my injuries. This hurt more than the rooster's pecks and scratches. As they applied the iodine on my back with the stiff plastic applicator, I squirmed liked a worm being impaled on a fish-hook. Chavela tried to distract me with one of her favorite say-ings. She said, "My husband *está tan viejo* [is so old], he doesn't let me buy him green bananas." She was laughing before she could finish the sentence, and I had no clue what she was talking about. The other one she liked to say was, "My *viejo* is so old, he knew the Dead Sea when it was sick."

Later that evening, Chavela and her husband, Eleazar, invited all of us to their house for dinner. Chavela had pre-pared for us some *arroz con pollo* (chicken with rice), in this case, it was *arroz con gallo* (rooster with rice). The meal was by far the best *dead* chicken I had ever tasted. We did not use napkins in those days. Everyone passed around a dish-drying towel. Before the meal, my mother told me and my two older brothers she did not want to hear a word out of us except for, "Thank you, Mr. and Mrs. Ramirez." We were on our best behavior. My oldest brother and I had been known to just look at each other and start laughing; even if it was during a rosary held at our house.

During the meal, Chavela enjoyed telling everyone the story of how she looked outside and saw the rooster scratching and pecking me on the ground. She was talking fast and would barely stop to take a breath. Her story was colorful, and she even threw in a few choice cuss words other than, "*gallo conde-nado.*" She went on to describe how much she enjoyed twisting the rooster's head off and pulling off his feathers con *ganas* (with *gusto*) while getting it ready for our meal.

When we finished eating, Chavela hugged me and told me I would not have to worry about the rooster anymore. She took me outside to show me the rooster's decapitated head that she had discarded in her back yard. I was afraid to get too close to the rooster's head because his eyes were bugged out and had a look of confusion. From a safe distance, I pointed at the rooster and stuck my tongue out; I laughed and yelled out, "Ha! Ha!" I hugged Chavela and told her, "Thank you for saving me, and the food was good too."

Later that night, before going to bed, I imitated the rooster one last time for my sister Lupe. She laughed as she saw me attempt to strut with a hunched, hurt back. At the end of the day, even though the rooster won the battle, I won the war (thanks to Chavela). This makes me more than a conqueror because I went to bed with a smile while burping rooster.

It was difficult to sleep that night because it was hot, and my back was irritated. My mind kept reliving the terror of being helpless against the rooster. I cried silently and wished I had obeyed my mother and stayed away from the rooster. Hmmm...maybe that's why the good book says, *"Children obey your parents in the Lord, for this pleases the Lord"* (Eph. 6:1 NIV).

Even today, more than 60 years later, Lupe will occasionally tease me by saying, "Hey Ruuster" instead of Ruben.

Earlier in the chapter, I left us with Adam and Eve kicked out of the Garden. So I must finish the story with a good ending, just like our last chapter in life. I want you to *get ready* now by fully trusting the plan God has for us.

Genesis 3:23 describes: *"So the Lord God banished him from the Garden of Eden to work the ground from which he had been taken. After he drove the man out, he placed on the east side of the Garden of Eden cherubim and a flaming sword flashing back and forth to guard the way to the tree of life."* All of us have been outside of the Garden ever since.

It is interesting for me to point out that before sending them out of the Garden, God in His goodness covered them in garments of skin. This is found in Genesis 3:21, *"The Lord God made garments of skin for Adam and his wife and clothed them."* This implies that the shedding of the first blood from an animal was used to cover their sin. Our sins are covered today by the blood of the Lamb. Always remember the proclamation from John the Baptist when he saw Jesus. He said, "Look, there He is, the Lamb of God, who takes away the sin of the world!" God's awesome plan to reconnect our souls to Him for eternity is made possible through the sacrifice of His only begotten Son, as described in John 3:16: *"For God so loved the world that he gave his one and only Son, that whoever believes in him shall not perish but have eternal life."* When we believe and surrender to the Lordship of Jesus, we no longer must hide. *"In His great mercy He has given us new birth into a living hope through the resurrection of Jesus Christ from the dead, and into an inheritance that can never perish, spoil or fade. This inheritance is kept in Heaven for you"* (1 Pet. 1:3–4).

**Eden Restored**—God's plan for us is contained all the way from the first book in the Bible when he banned Adam and Eve from the Garden of Eden by saying, *"The man has now become like one of us, knowing good and evil. He must not be allowed to reach out his hand and take also from <u>the tree of life</u> and eat, and live forever"* (Gen. 3:22). I underlined "the tree of life" to show you where this tree is and that it still exists, as told in the last book of the Bible. In Revelation 22:2 it describes part of Heaven, *"On each side of the river stood the tree of life, bearing twelve crops of fruit, yielding its fruit every month. And the leaves are for the healing of the nations."* How about that! I can hardly wait to eat from the tree of life.

To further my point on God's plan for us to be reconciled to him I use scripture, not my words but those inspired to Paul

36

by the Holy Spirit. *"Consequently, just as one trespass resulted in condemnation for all people, so also one righteous act resulted in justification and life for all people. For just as through the disobedience of the one man the many were made sinners, so also through the obedience of the one man the many will be made righteous"* (Rom. 5:18–19). It is plain to see the one disobedient man is Adam and the one obedient man is our Lord and Savior, Jesus Christ. The offer of life through Jesus remains for us all. Thank you, Father, for this simple plan of salvation. Our only way to get us into eternity with you. As for me and my house, we will serve the Lord for the remainder of our days. I am Heaven-bound! *Will I see you at the Tree?*

I was born again into the army of God at age 47 after being seasoned with 30 years of alcohol. I accepted Jesus as my Lord and Savior on November 13, 1999, at Primera Baptist Church. My new "drill instructor" was named Diana Tello, who was well versed in the good book. She only spoke Spanish, and my heart and soul absorbed every word like a thirsty cactus after a much-needed rain. I kept asking her when I would be baptized, and she would just say, *"Solo Dios sabe"* ("Only God knows"). After a couple of months, she asked me, *"Ruben, ¿qué es bueno?"* (What is good?). I was puzzled by the question, and again she asked me to tell her what good is.

I thought to myself, "This is it, the final quiz that will get me immersed into the baptismal font." I quickly proceeded to tell all the things of how I define "good." She repeated, *"¿Y qué más?"* (What else?) several times. I must have talked for 15 minutes and told her about everything from praying to helping the elderly cross the street. I even mentioned picking up the tab when at lunch or dinner with someone. Finally, I reached, my last item, which was about calling my mom regularly. She had a sly smile and said, "Okay, open your Bible and go to the verse found in James 4:17." It says, "*If anyone, then, knows the good they ought to do and doesn't do it, it is sin for them.*" She smiled and said, "You know what is good, and I know you don't want to sin." My old self was screaming, "You are wrong for doing that!" As a new creation in Christ, I knew that spiritually it was the best for me.

So here is the question: What is good? Write your complete list of what is good and then stop sinning!

During an extended work assignment in Washington, DC, I loaned my prized possession to a young man. Billy was in Texas and was unable to rent a car because he was under the age of 25. I told him to take my 1997 Buick Riviera from my garage and use it for his out-of-town job interview. My son Anthony was still in Texas and gave him the keys to the car that was not supposed to be moved until I came home. Anthony was quick to point out that I had told him not to move the car during my absence.

Early the next morning as I was getting ready for work, Billy called me and told me he had hit a deer with my car. It stopped me in my tracks, and right away I told him, "Wait a minute, I'll call you back!" I got off the phone and went into an angry rant as I told Irma what I had just heard. She told me to calm down, and she asked me whether Billy had been hurt. To my amazement, I said, "I don't know." She reassured me the car could be restored. After jumping up and down and being verbally upset, I composed myself enough to call him back. Billy felt horrible, as he told me what had happened again. I was able to get the words out, "I'm glad you did not get hurt! We can get the car fixed later." I am thankful that I did not say anything to Billy that morning that would have ruined our relationship. Once the words come out, you can't put them back in your mouth. Hurtful words are like an echo in the ears of our souls that never go away. A bruise will go away; harsh words are permanent.

I am also thankful that when I need God, He doesn't say, "Wait a minute, I'll call you back!" like I did to Billy that morning. God is always there for us. We just need to take His Hand and walk in obedience. God is our Shepherd; He is our Leader that nudges us sheep in the direction He wants us to go. (More on Psalm 23 in the next chapter.) If we get lost along the way, He will leave the other sheep until He finds the one. "Doesn't He leave the ninety-nine in the open country and go after the lost sheep until He finds it?" (Lk. 15:4).

It is my hope the scriptures in *Golden Walk* are coating your heart and soul like sun protection lotion. Consider them as a form of heat insurance as it is mighty hot down there. This Son protection lotion has an SPF factor of 3:16.

**SPF-3:16 stands for:**

reduced <u>S</u>tress, improved <u>P</u>eace, and increased <u>F</u>aith **3:16.** Apply it to your ***heart*** abundantly!

*"I have hidden Your Word in my <u>heart</u> that I might not sin against You"* (Ps. 119:11).

**Golden Step #3: If you know what is good and you don't do it, you sin.**

# CHAPTER 4

*"Surely Your <u>Goodness and Love</u> will follow me all the days of my life, and I will dwell in the house of the Lord forever"* (Ps. 23:6).

Life can be hard, and when tough times come, we need some solid scripture to stand on. Psalm 23 is one of my favorites to rely on. It helps to have those go-to scriptures when you are walking through the darkest valley and you need that extra push to get out of the shadow of darkness. When we have a strong leader, He (shepherd) guides us so we stay on the right path. Make sure to find a good leader with a solid moral compass. One that follows sound doctrine *instead of* someone who teaches what itching ears want to hear.

**Psalm 23** is a masterpiece as the shepherd leads us to quiet waters to refresh our souls and we fear no evil. When the wolf comes to devour, you need a pit bull or two to protect the flock. At the end of this awesome Psalm, there are two sheepdogs following the flock; their names are *Goodness and Love*. Not only do they protect us, but they follow us all the days of our lives until we dwell in the house of the Lord forever. What a beautiful picture as we journey through life!

*A psalm of David.*
*The L*ORD *is my shepherd, I lack nothing.*
*He makes me lie down in green pastures, He leads me beside quiet waters,*
*He refreshes my soul. He guides me along the right paths for His name's sake.*
*Even though I walk through the darkest valley, I will fear no evil, for You are with me; your rod and your staff, they comfort me.*
*You prepare a table before me in the presence of my enemies. You anoint my head with oil; my cup overflows.*
*Surely your goodness and love will follow me all the days of my life, and I will dwell in the house of the L*ORD *forever.*

## A Dog Named Champ

As I mentioned earlier, when I was a young boy I had a paper route. Delivering newspapers in the early morning darkness in the barrio always provided some unique challenges. There were times when I had to out-pedal a dog that wanted to see what I tasted like. My relief came when I began taking my dog named Champ along with me for protection. He was extremely protective of me but sometimes got me in trouble. One day when I was collecting for the newspaper service, Champ busted through a screen door to teach a yappy chihuahua a lesson. It caused a big commotion as Champ went through the screen door and quieted this little dog that was full of chaos and courage. The woman in the house was busy making tortillas, and her three children were watching *The Wallace and Ladmo Show* on television. I had a difficult time dragging Champ out of their house. My father had to repair their screen, and "Yappy" never bothered me again. The husband, who owned the house, later told me, "It's about time someone shut that dog up."

Champ was an awesome dog, and in my corny style I would brag about him. I told my friends that Champ could talk. They said, "Yeah, right." I told them when I ask Champ what his favorite bird is, he'd reply, "Owwll!" If I ask him, "What's on top of the house?" he'll say "Roof!" And finally, if I ask him, "How does it feel when you sit on coarse sandpaper?" He'll reply, "Ruff!" I told you it was corny.

One day my father was going to Moe's Food Fair Market (later renamed Carlito's) and asked me if I wanted to go with him. That's like asking a squirrel if it wants an acorn. He told me Champ would have to stay home. I jumped in the back of the truck, and as the truck started to move forward, I gave Champ an undetected, low whistle. Champ was athletic enough to jump into the back of the truck as my father was pulling away.

When we got to Moe's Food Fair Market, my father was upset and told me he had said he did not want the dog to come. I said, "He jumped in, and I could not stop him." My father said, "He better not come into the store." I scolded Champ and told him to stay put in the back of the truck. As we were walking through the store aisles, we heard some commotion from the butcher area. Champ had made his way into the store and helped himself to a hefty serving of ground beef from behind the glass counter. The butcher chased Champ with a broom and yelled, "Whose dog is this?" Champ had red ground beef all over his snout and ran next to my father for protection. The butcher asked my father, "Is this your dog?" Suddenly, my father could not speak English and said, "*Yo no sé inglés*" ("I don't know English"). I quickly chased Champ from inside the store back to my father's truck. It was hilarious! I knew I had to get my dog out of there quickly, before I fell from laughter.

"Big Trouble" was coming home in the truck with us. It was written all over the scowl my father had on his face as he drove home. It relieved me when my father started laughing unexpectedly. He shook his head while saying, "What are we going to do with this dog?" I should have renamed Champ *Big Trouble* as he later in life managed to bite the mailman, kill a duck, pull a passing motorcycle rider off his bike, and survive being hit by a car.

Champ was temporary protection; he died, and I lost his protection. Nothing can separate us from the love and fortification provided by God. *"For I am convinced that neither death nor life, neither the present nor the future, nor any powers, neither height nor depth, nor anything else in all creation, will be able to separate us from the love of God that is Christ Jesus our Lord"* (Rom. 8:38–39).

## In the Hollow of His Hand

"Who has measured the waters in the *hollow of His hand* or with the breadth of his hand marked off the heavens? Who has held the dust of the earth in a basket, or weigh the mountains on the scales and the hills in a balance?" (Isa. 40:12).

God is all-powerful and all-present. God can measure the waters of the entire earth in the hollow of His Hand and with the breadth of those Hands. Take a moment and look at the palm of your hand. Curl your fingers in such a manner that you can hold water in the hollow of your hand. Not much fits, right? Now stretch out your hand as wide as you can; mine doesn't even mark off my entire mouse pad or size of my Bible. After spending time in deep blue waters in the Navy and on multiple cruises, it is difficult for me to comprehend the sovereignty and unfathomable size of God. It is mind-boggling for me to try to grasp that our Creator can hold all the oceans on earth in the *hollow of His Hand.*

It was an honor for me to serve our country onboard a Navy ship that became my floating home for two years. We traveled twice to an area halfway across the world during my two deployments in 1972 and 1973. My ship, the USS Gray, was a destroyer; it was 438 feet long (almost the length of one and a half football fields) and weighed 4066 tons. It was relatively small when compared to other naval warships. The ship probably looked like a piece of straw in the ocean from God's viewpoint. Our boat carried a crew of thirteen officers and 211 enlisted men. God took care of us in the *hollow of His Hand* as I had the privilege of serving on two West Pacific tours (seven months each) of duty. During those two years we spent most of our time providing naval gun fire support to the ground soldiers in Vietnam. God watched over us in the high seas when we had to replenish more shells and powder for our guns. The work was strenuous as we had to form a human chain to pass heavy canisters of powder and 50-pound shells used for firing. We usually took on additional ammunition about twice a week. It was tough to maintain our balance as we passed the ammo while the ship rocked. This was strenuous for the arms but great for the abs. They say, "Rough seas make good sailors."

Toward the end of my second tour of Vietnam, we were allowed to go swimming in the middle of the ocean. We had been on the ship for over 60 days without stepping on land. We were on our way for some rest and relaxation when we received orders to change plans and had to sail unexpectedly to Karachi, Pakistan. We were not allowed to go ashore in Pakistan, and when we were finished with our mission, the ship headed for open seas. I never knew what our mission was, and I just went for the ride like some ABC (already been chewed) gum on the bottom of your shoe. The ship stopped after a few hours, and we dropped anchor. We were given permission to jump off the ship for an afternoon swim in the middle of the Indian Ocean. *What a once-in-a-lifetime experience!* Even though I was in tip-top condition, I only jumped off and climbed back on the ship three times because it was so exhausting. We had to climb the side of the ship using netting. This would be equivalent to climbing on a net to the top of a two-story house that is wet and rocking. A few of the guys climbed to higher decks and made beautiful dives into the ocean. I had enough wisdom to jump in feet first and then alternated between dog paddling and back floating to conserve energy.

There were many of my shipmates who chose not to go swimming. It makes me wonder if they regret missing the opportunity to take that plunge. It was rather eerie to jump into the water. I could not help but think about sharks getting ready to have me as an appetizer. It made me get "goosies" from my scalp to the soles of my feet. I never felt completely comfortable that our protection came from a few crew members onboard the captain's boat circling our group of swimmers. I remember our protectors standing and looking in the water intently from the small boat. They were armed with loaded rifles ready to shoot hungry sharks. I'm sure none of them had ever been to a shooting range where the targets had a shark painted on it. (I'm forever thankful that God was and still is our Protector.) I quickly calmed myself by figuring out: if I am not the slowest swimmer to the net, I will be okay. The other mental struggle was thinking about staying afloat in the deepest water I had ever been in. The Indian Ocean water is virtually bottomless. I kept looking down into the water to see if there was anything swimming underneath me. It seemed like at any moment something would bump against you. Even my own dog paddling legs touching together sent what felt like electricity going up my spine. Looking back, we survived it because we were swimming in the *hollow of His Hand*.

*"When you pass through the waters, I will be with you; and when you pass through the rivers, they will not sweep over you. When you walk through the fire, you will not be burned; the flames will not set you ablaze. For I am the Lord your God, the Holy One of Israel, your Savior"* (Isa. 43:2–3).

That scripture will get rid of the bogeyman and *La Llorona*. Nothing can harm us because we are secure in the *hollow of His Hand*.

As you increase your belief in the Word of God, you must develop unshakable faith knowing God will provide all that you need. *"When you ask, you must believe and not doubt, because the one who doubts is like a wave of the sea, blown and tossed in the wind"* (Jm. 1:6).

## Getting into His Word

It is wonderful to get up early and search for nuggets that can be found in the Bible from Genesis to Revelation. Recently, I read a verse in the book of Genesis where God has completed the sixth day of Creation. This comes after God has created mankind in His image. *"God saw all He had made and God saw it was very good. And there was evening, and there was morning – the sixth day"* (Gen. 1:31). When I saw it, it made me say, "Goodness!" Okay, no big deal—until you realize that God on the previous five days of Creation, at the end of each day, saw that it *was good*.

It made me contemplate the word "good." The dictionary defines good (when used as a noun) as follows: "that which is morally right; a mysterious balance of good and evil." So why *good* for five days and *very good* after the sixth day? Maybe because God now had infused His Breath of Life into every living creature that moves along the ground. Can you think of a single word that is better than good? God in His goodness gave us the simple answer: *very good*. Check it out for yourself in the Creation story in the first book.

The continuation of the story in Genesis features Adam and Eve and their disobedience. They made a bad choice that separated them and mankind from God. Thousands of years later God sends His only begotten Son to reconcile us to Him. Whosoever believes in His Son will not perish but have eternal life. When I chose to accept Jesus as my Lord and Savior at age 47, I used to worry that I would not be able to stop drinking alcohol. I had been drinking for 30 years. It was only through the grace of God that this addiction was taken from me. Goodness gracious! It has been over 21 years now.

Over the years, I have contemplated the verse in Ecclesiastes 2:14 *"The wise have eyes in their heads, while the fool walks in darkness."* I could not make sense of this until recently. The answer came to me by examining this in the spiritual sense. The wise have eyes in their head as they know Jesus and have the blessed assurance of where they will spend eternity. The light in their heads is the truth in their brain. Nothing else matters! The fool walks in darkness in a continuous search for the truth and the light of the world. It is such a blessing to know I am good to go at the end of this earthly life.

Look at our supposed leaders, and see who they walk with, what are their values. Their actions and words will shine light on the darkness.

Becoming Christian is as easy as ABC as outlined in these Bible verses:

A. "All have sinned and come short of the Glory of God" (Rom. 3:23; 6:23; 1 Jn. 1:10).

B. "Believe on the Lord Jesus Christ, and you will be saved" (Acts 16:31; Jn. 1:12).

C. "If you confess with your mouth that Jesus is Lord and believe in your heart that God raised Him from the dead, you will be saved (Rom. 10:9; Eph. 2:8–9).

## Let the Lamb Make the Reservation, Not the bunny

Easter Sunday has been one of my favorite days for as long as I can remember. As a child, it was all about the Easter bunny, hiding Easter eggs, and having a great time with the family all day. All the attention was on the bunny bringing us a basket to use during the Easter egg hunt with our cousins. We dressed in our best clothes and had pictures taken of us with squinting eyes as the Arizona sun was so bright. One of the things about going to a restaurant after church service on Easter is you will have to wait, even when you have a reservation.

As a child of God, my focus has changed, and now I celebrate the Lamb of God rather than a bunny. The Good News about Easter is Jesus has resurrected and has cleansed us of our sins so we can get to Heaven. The Better News is He is *coming back* for us; He is *praying* for us in Heaven, and He is *preparing a place* for us without us having to make a reservation. There will be no waiting or squinting eyes.

All we must do is believe. He said it, *"I am the Way, the Truth and the Life, no one comes to the Father except through me"* (Jn. 14:6). In Romans 10: 9 it says: *"If you confess with your mouth the Lord Jesus and believe in your heart that God raised him from the dead, you will be saved."* It's that simple; it is the free gift to get into Heaven without a reservation.

Make sure your name is on the list to get into Heaven. It must be written in the Lamb's Book of Life. There will be no waiting because *the Lamb made the reservation, not the bunny.*

## A Changed Heart

After I accepted Jesus as Lord and Savior, there was a new song in my heart. The song fit right in with the beating of my heart. Did you know your heart beats about 100,000 times per day or 36,500,000 per year?[3] Just thinking about this makes my head get itchy; then I have this urge to scratch my balding head. Thinking about all those heart beats also makes me feel tired.

As a young man I tried to influence the world with the music I listened to: Motown, Beatles, Three Dog Night, Chicago, and so forth. The louder, the better! Now as a "seasoned, wiser man," I do not listen to loud music, but I hear a continuous song in my heart with no lyrics. It has calmed my overall well-being and provides nourishment to my soul. Food for our soul is more important than food for our body.

I read in Proverbs 9:3 how wisdom called out from the highest point in the city ."*Leave your simple [means foolish] ways and you will live; walk in the way of insight*" (Prov. 9:6). Wisdom taught me to listen to the music that comes only from Jesus. This music makes me dance to the beat of a different Drummer; The One who is way better than Ringo Starr. That reminds me of a comment John Lennon made when asked if Ringo was the greatest drummer in the world. John quickly responded, "He is not even the best drummer in the Beatles."

Have you ever stopped to think about the ways God takes care of us without us having to think about it? For example, we don't have to tell our heart to beat or command our lungs to breathe in and out. God made a special part of the body called the medulla oblongata, (M.O.).[4] (Sounds like a word from the movie Lion King.) The M.O. is a part of the brain that is located at the top of our spinal cords. It acts like a letter carrier that delivers messages to all parts of the body. It controls breathing, your heartbeat, and also your blood pressure. The M.O. takes care of all that and also controls coughing, sneezing, and swallowing. God takes care of us in ways we never thank Him for. Take time to count your blessings and give Him thanks. Make sure to thank Him for those fingers you are counting your blessings on. Say thanks for the ability to count. Be grateful that you can always count on Him. God has blessed us in so many ways — have you ever wondered about how many different smells our nose can remember? I got curious and asked Siri — the answer is about a trillion (unless you are nosey — just kidding).

My life changed as I read, *"The fear of the Lord is the beginning of knowledge, but fools despise wisdom and instruction"* (Prov. 1:7). Fear in this scripture is not about being scared or frightened. It is about being in awe and giving reverence to our Almighty God. As I immersed myself in the living water of the four gospels, I gained knowledge and understanding from our Lord's example. I have grown to know what really matters in life, that is, to love God and love people. If you close your eyes and know the song, you can almost hear Danny Gokey singing that lyric.

Life is surrounded by people who judge us day in and day out. They will not acknowledge us when we succeed but laugh when we fail. They think that their words and opinions can make us or break us. My purpose is now to live a humble life that pleases God until He calls me Home. My soul is set on a direct course toward Heaven.

You will not hear loud music blasting from my vehicle anymore. My hope is to crank up the volume from the song and joy in my heart as I put it on paper. My changed heart plays a continuous song without my knowledge of the lyrics. Several years ago, I prayed for revelation of my utterances from within when speaking in the Heavenly language. The answer came back as: *"Better is one day in your courts than a thousand elsewhere"* (Ps. 84:10).

Take time to be joyful when you lift songs of praise even if you can't carry a tune in a bucket. When it is sincere, God is pleased with our gratitude. Perhaps your singing will uplift whoever is in your household. I love to hear Irma when she gets lost in her songs of praise and worship. Her singing is like candy for my ears, and I usually join in, but my singing is usually just a hair off key. You must know your strengths, so here I am typing words on the keyboard while humming.

I pray to receive wisdom to enhance my writing to glorify Him magnificently. May the words that come from my innermost thoughts be pleasing to Him and serve to increase our faith. God has given me the wonderful blessing of being able to write. Most importantly, He provides the wisdom to understand that my writing is for the Glory of God alone. My purpose for the remainder of my life is to tell others about Jesus. The goal of this book is to help reduce your **S**tress on earth, improve your **P**eace in daily life, and increase your **F**aith using scripture, with **SPF 3:16.** We must believe in His Son so we do not perish but have eternal life.

**Golden Step #4: Goodness and Love will follow us all the way into Heaven.**

# CHAPTER 5

## THE BREAD OF GOD

*"For <u>the bread of God</u> is the bread that comes down from heaven and gives life to the world"* (Jn. 6:33).

The meaning of Jesus's life was to be our gift; the purpose of His life was to give it away. Christ is our perfect Gift because God loved us so much, He gave us His only begotten Son. Jesus fulfilled His purpose in life when He gave it all away for us on the Cross.

It was all done on purpose: *"For the bread of God is the bread that comes down from heaven and gives life to the world"* (Jn. 6:33). *"In him [Jesus] was life, and that Life was the light of all mankind"* (Jn. 1:4). Now it's time to celebrate the remainder of your life in a special way.

This must be done on purpose. Accept the Gift of Christ as your Lord and Savior. Be part of the chosen people, God's special possession, so we can praise Him for eternity. He has taken us out of the darkness and into His wonderful light. It's the best gift you will ever receive in your life and then do something else on purpose: Give the Gift away by sharing Him with others.

"The meaning of life is to find your gift … the purpose of life is to give it away." — Pablo Picasso[5]

## No Blueberries in the Barrio

Then Jesus declared, *"I am the bread of life. Whoever comes to me will never go hungry, and whoever believes in me will never be thirsty"* (Jn. 6:35).

My prayer today is this short story will be like a river flowing to nourish the root system of your heart. Flowing into your soul like those canals I used to swim in that provided much-needed water in the Valley of the Sun.

Growing up "south of the tracks" in Phoenix, Arizona, I didn't have some of the things that I do now. Just to name a few, there were *no blueberries in the barrio*. Now I eat them almost every day, mixed in with my yogurt to keep me full of antioxidants and regular (it works for me). These little plump, bluish-purple small pillows of fruity flavor are incredible. I did not get to eat a bagel with cream cheese until age 24 and sushi swam into my mouth (thank God) at age 39. We did not have pajamas in the 'hood; however, when you do not have these things, you can't miss something that does not exist in your world.

Please do not think I am looking for sympathy — put down those violins, stop that sad music. We were poor, but trust me, I always had way more than I needed growing up in the barrio. We had an abundance of figs, mulberries, pomegranates, nopales, verdolagas, and occasionally pecans.

My Tio Pancho would climb that tall tree and shake it with all his might while he yelled "Charracate! Charracate!" I'm not sure what that word meant; maybe it was passed down from our Aztec ancestors. The word "charracate!" seemed to give him the strength of a chango (orangutan). Unlimited pecans hit us as we stood underneath the tree. We had more pecans than you could shake a tree at.

So what is my point? I want to fill you in on where I was undernourished in the barrio. I did not get to establish a personal relationship with Jesus until age 47, and my father did not make his decision until he was near the end of his life, at the age of 78.

My father used to tease one of my friends named Arturo. He would call him, "Arturo, *pan duro!*" It rhymes in Spanish and means, Arthur, hard bread. Arturo would get annoyed and asked me, "Why is your dad always hassling me?" My father would laugh and finish by saying, "*El pan no es duro …duro es no tener pan!*" ("the bread is not hard; it is hard not to have bread"). He always reminded us how difficult life was when he had to work in the fields from sunrise to sunset instead of being able to go to school. I remember asking him if they took breaks, and he said only when it was time to eat. I knew they probably did not wear wrist watches, and I asked him about how they knew when it was time to eat. He said they would place a large stick into the ground, and when there was no shadow, it was time to eat. With my appetite, I would have been keeping a close eye on that branch, and my new nickname would have been Ruben Stick Watcher.

***Bonus fact***: *The world's largest sundial is the Vrihat Samrat Yantra, which was built in Jaipur, India, in 1738. It is nearly 90 feet tall and is accurate to within two seconds. The shadow moves about one millimeter (about the thickness of a dime) every second. The name means "the great king of instruments."*[6]

During a recent morning walk while I was enjoying my time with God, I heard the words, *"El pan no es duro ... duro es no tener pan!"* My paradigm got shifted when I thought about this in the spiritual sense. The undernourishment I had in the barrio came from not getting a full portion of the Bread of Life. It was evident in my father's words when he received salvation. After I read him the story in John chapter 14, he received just what he needed at that moment. When we got to John 14:6, *"Jesus answered, 'I am the Way and the Truth and the Life. No one comes to the father except through me,'"* my father looked amazed and said, "So that's where that comes from?" We had only received crumbs by getting part of the bread (Word of God) most of our lives. Most of our church life we only heard or read "I am the Way" without knowing the full story. I asked my papa if he wanted to hear more, and he said, "Yes!" We continued trotting down a path that is called the Roman route (this a series of scriptures that begins in the book of Romans). My father made a personal connection with Jesus as Lord and Savior that day! Alleluia! If you get a chance, read about this in the last chapter of *Barrio Walk: Stepping into Wisdom*. It is the greatest miracle I have ever experienced.

At age 47, I heard the words in John 6:54 NIV: Jesus said, *"Whoever eats my flesh and drinks my blood has eternal life, and I will raise them up at the last day."* What an awesome promise! Back in those days when Jesus was walking on our Earth, his words were extremely controversial. He lost many followers because those listening to him only knew of what was being taught in the Law by the Pharisees. Many thought Jesus was off his rocker when they thought about eating physically from His Flesh and Blood. Some people also stop listening to me when I talk about Jesus being the only way to the Father. I grew up reciting the Apostle's Creed at Our Lady of Fatima and still believe most of that prayer.

I am heaven-bound with a renewed heart to go with my balding head. When I decided to follow Christ, he yanked me out of the darkness that was fueled by alcohol for 30 years. He put me on the path to peace fully clothed and in my right mind. My mind is now centered, and my heart is finally calm. I no longer must go to a man to confess my sins; I communicate with Jesus directly. *"There is One God and One Mediator between God and man, the Man Christ Jesus"* (1 Tim. 2:5 NIV).

I want you to go to Heaven with me. If you are undernourished, like I was, I will be glad to help you on this journey. We do not need blueberries, sushi, bagels, or nopales—we need our Daily Bread. I am going to leave you with something to chew on until the next chapter. Read this carefully: *If you are not seated at the Lord's table eating the Bread of Life, you might find yourself on Satan's menu.*

## The Manna

After the Israelites had fled from Egypt and crossed the parted Red Sea, they grumbled to Moses and his brother Aaron. They said, *"If only we had died by the Lord's hand in Egypt! There we sat around pots of meat and ate all the food we wanted, but you have brought us out into this desert to starve this entire assembly to death"* (Ex. 16:3). God heard them and, in His goodness, sent down bread from heaven with specific instructions to test them. Each day the Israelites were to gather enough (an omer per person) for each day. What is an omer? It is an ancient Hebrew unit of dry measure equal to a tenth of an ephah, about 3.5 liters (3.7 quarts). It is an offering of a sheaf or an omer of the first harvest of barley to a priest in the Temple on the second day of Passover.[7] On the sixth day they were to gather twice as much, as there would be none sent down on the Sabbath. The bread God sent down from Heaven was called manna. It was white like coriander seed and tasted like wafers made with honey.

When the Israelites gathered more than an omer per person (about two quarts) and kept some until the following morning, it became full of maggots and began to smell badly. The Israelites got tired of eating manna, and they grumbled ungratefully.

There have been occasions in life when I 'gathered' more than I needed. When I lived in McAllen, Texas, I would exclaim, "Tacos!" and stop at different locations during my commute home from work. After two years of this delicious eating, my weight and pant size set personal all-time highs. I had to buy more clothes and belts.

All my life, my mother has told me, "You need to stop eating so much!" I just happen to hold the Gonzales household record of eating 17 tacos at a single meal. It came during my Phoenix college days after some rigorous games of basketball at University Park. A few years ago, when my mother visited me in Texas, she looked at a street sign near my house, which is Murchinson Ridge Road. She called it Munchingson Ridge and said, "You need to stop eating so much." It makes me chuckle regularly as I need to pass this sign almost daily on the drive to my house.

*Gluttony* is one of the seven deadly sins as I was rudely reminded when I checked into a restaurant on Facebook. My immediate response to this comment was, "So is *envy*. Boom!" Is desiring more than you have or need a sin? When I was addicted to gambling, I would many times end up losing because of my *greed* for wanting more. (Wow, without much effort, I have touched on three of the seven deadly sins.) At this point, I know you are wondering about the four other deadly sins, so here they are: *pride, lust, wrath,* and *sloth.*

The large jackpot hit at the beginning of a gambling night can easily dwindle down to nothing and then some. I used to love to play blackjack and spent many hours at the third base position on the table. My goal was to make the dealer say, "Purple out," which means a $500 chip was being given to me when I cashed out. My addiction made me bet the purple chip on one hand on two different occasions. I lost the first time but won on my second attempt. There is a nervous anticipation that is hard to describe as you await the fate of your purple chip. I tried to remain emotionless and appear fearless on a big bet. The saying from the hood is, "Scared money don't make no money!"

Those few moments make your heart reach its target rate as you wait to see the outcome of your hand. I always did my darndest not to show any emotion, win or lose. With the turn of the card, it is over. It is an adrenaline rush that I pray I never experience again.

The same went with drinking alcohol; if I drank more than two, the forecast called for a heavy downpour and a night of bad decisions. It's where I used to be and makes me more grateful that I will never be there again. How can I be so confident that I will never be there again? The scripture in 2 Peter 2:22 says, *"A dog returns to its vomit."* Fortunately for me, I am not a dog, I am a new creation in Christ. However, I recently came home from a glamping vacation with a tick attached to the back of my knee. Who says you can't show an old dog (me) new ticks? LOL

## The Record Snowfall in Pflugerville

Early in 2021, Texas experienced some of the harshest weather ever. It was the most cold weather I have ever been in for an extended period. The loss of electricity affects so many of the everyday conveniences that we take for granted. I wrote about this experience before the snow melted while it was fresh on my mind. This was not to complain but to document how getting through this increased our faith and made us more grateful. Here is a list of what we lost and how we accommodated.

| What we lost | How we accommodated |
|---|---|
| 1. Electricity (no Keurig) | 2. Heated water on gas stove, instant coffee |
| 3. Toasted bread | 4. Tortilla placed on the stove flame |
| 5. Heat | 6. More clothes and gas burner from stove |
| 7. Oven for baking | 8. Propane grill made awesome chicken wings |
| 9. TV for entertainment | 10. Made snow angels, danced, sang, and played cards |
| 11. Bible app on iPhone | 12. Read from first Bible with handwritten notes |
| 13. Water for flushing | 14. Melted snow on gas stove |
| 15. Light | 16. Used candles and flashlights |
| 17. Communication | 18. Recharge of phone using vehicle charging method |
| 19. Gym | 20. Shoveling snow is a strenuous workout |

| 21. No computer for writing | 22. Miss Sharon taught me to write in cursive in 1959 |
|---|---|

**Lessons learned in the dark and cold**. Give thanks in all circumstances (1 Thess. 5:18). This too shall pass. Get the snow and ice off your path so you do not slip or fall. Make sure there are no things in the way so you do not stumble in the dark. "Your word is Lamp to my feet!" (Ps. 119:105). Prepare for hard times with lots of drinking water, candles, and propane. Check on your neighbors. Be an encouragement, praise loud, and never lose faith. Stay positive in tough times. As a man thinks, so he is; there is no good or bad, only thinking makes it so. Remember, the Son will always shine, and all you really need is beans and rice and Jesus Christ.

It made me learn that having a gas stove in the house is much like having a four-wheel drive vehicle for the snow. You can get through the snow and cold weather, but it makes it easier with a gas stove. If I ever must buy another vehicle, four-wheel drive is an absolute requirement.

During the darkest and coldest hours, I was not able to use my Bible app. This meant I could not conveniently hear or read from my iPad. I pulled out my first Bible and found a note that lifted my spirits. The flashlight was shining brightly as it illuminated my handwritten notes to myself. I wrote it when I was a brand-new Christian, 21 years ago. "Be bold, be happy, be strong, be brave, be sweet, be free, be original...but most importantly, BE YOU!" This encouraged me to make a snow angel while wearing cowboy boots. I tried to build a snowman, but the snow was too powdery, so I made a snow volcano; I used yellow spray paint and *Cholula* for lava. When cold and age prevent you from completing your snow man, get creative, and make a snow volcano. This comes with this caveat: Never, ever eat yellow snow!

I made my first snow angel at age 68.

One evening we entertained ourselves by playing black-jack by candlelight. I tried hard to figure out how to win all the pinto beans as I dealt cards to Irma and my sister Anita. It was all in fun to watch them count as they added my 6 cards that totaled 22. This came after I had just announced my hand total was 21. It's hard to cheat when you are playing UNO. In the dark and shadows of the indirect light, I was able to sneak in a blue card when the color being played was green. We laughed and made up victory cheers. My chant went "ROO! ROO! BEN! BEN!" as I raised my hands toward Heaven after my insignificant victory. It was all for amusement and for our sanity. It made the day go by just a hair quicker and made a special memory.

We were dealing with the dark and cold as best we could. Then, some more bad news came, no water was coming out of our kitchen faucet. Oh no! None out of the other faucets in the house either. I could not understand it as I had covered the outside spigots and detached the water hoses. My mind raced to broken pipes and plumbing costs. Because we had no communication, I did not know the city had shut off the water supply. As I prayed worried about how to have water for toilet flushing, bingo, I thought, "Melt some snow." Isn't it wonderful how God gives you solutions when when you pray?". . . *in all things God works for the good of those who love Him, who have been called according to His purpose"* (Rom. 8:28).

It was a relief when the city announced water was going to flow again after a couple of days. The hot shower felt wonderful after not having a hot shower for four days. Ahh! Cleanliness is next to godliness!

When the snowfall started falling, it looked like manna coming down from the sky. It is amazing that God creates each tiny snowflake uniquely. I was blessed to see a snowflake with all its custom features while sitting on an airplane on a cold morning in Washington, DC. Here is a stanza from a poem called "Just for Us." Special note: you will find the full poem with explanation in the afterword section of this book.

*Little snowflake landing on the window*
*Displaying all of its uniqueness*
*Praising God with your one-of-a-kind features*
*Created by the Father*
*Just for a moment*
*Just like us*

Snowfall-inspired poetry by my wife, Irma, is shown below:

Have you ever heard a snowflake fall?
Has a snowflake ever landed on your hand?
And you admire its beauty?
Have you ever tasted a snowflake?

Was it sweet, did it tickle?
If you put several together in your mouth
Would they crunch?
Have you ever thanked God for snowflakes?
Has He ever received the praise for making
Each snowflake perfect and unique from the other?
The perfect color of the snowflake, white
As white as the Lamb is pure
No stains, no abnormalities,
Just a perfect little snowflake.
Perfect, just like us, with a clean and pure color
As we enter the gates of Heaven
Perfect like a new creation He's created in us
Born to do only one thing, to serve him.
Thank you, Lord, for the snowflakes
Thank you for letting us experience
This perfect creation
With your help, some day when I grow up
I want to be just like that snowflake
Perfect, standing before you, my Savior

Before leaving this portion of the book, I learned you must be extra careful when shoveling snow and ice. I can't afford the embarrassment or bill from falling down and breaking a hip. I discovered sometimes there were footprints of ice where someone had walked on the sidewalk. Their weight compressed the snow and each step they had taken became frozen ice. These frozen footsteps made it more treacherous as you can't detect them and you unexpectedly lose your footing while trying to maintain traction to shovel. The whole experience of being shut down in the house increased our faith and trust in God. My hope is this part of the book leaves small tracks of faith engrained in your heart.

## House of Bread

Did you know that the word "Bethlehem" means "house of bread"? It is awesome how God sent his Son, the Bread of Life, to be born in a town whose name means house of bread and then had Him born in complete humility in a manger. If I would have been Jesus, my announcement to the world would have included lots of bling, fireworks, and acknowledgment. Maybe landing on earth on a rocket or driven to my birth site in a pearl-white Maserati. Maybe I would have had a song blaring like "Celebration" by Kool and Gang or lots of horns being played by Tower of Power. Thank you, Jesus, for stepping out of Heaven and bringing Your Light into the darkness of the world.

I'm glad the visit from the Magi included gifts of gold and of incense and of myrrh, even though it all belonged to Jesus already. We will never repay You enough for the sacrifice You made for us after coming down from Heaven. This was just the beginning, and He'll be back. The star displayed by God lit up the sky with some heavenly bling and led the three kings and shepherds to the manger. The shepherds were terrified when an angel appeared to them and said, *Do not be afraid. I bring news of great joy that will be for all the people"* (Lk. 2:10). Then a great company of a heavenly choir appeared and praised God, "Glory to God in the highest, and on earth peace to men on whom His favor rests" (Lk. 2:14). Now, that is a God-sent arrival that is way better than a worldly band, fireworks, or coming to earth on a rocket.

Why was Jesus born in Bethlehem? According to Luke, Joseph and Mary's trip to Bethlehem was to satisfy an imperial command by Caesar Augustus that all individuals return to their ancestral towns, that all the world should be taxed. That way everyone could be accounted for and then pay their taxes. Our world would be a better place if we did not have to pay taxes or interest. Our best world will come when we finally take that Golden Walk in Heaven. God always has a better plan for us than we do. Put complete trust in Him. Remember, sometimes *good things fall apart so better things can fall together.*

**Golden Step #5: The bread of God gives us eternal life, only if we believe.**

# CHAPTER 6

## REPENT AND BELIEVE THE GOOD NEWS!

*"The time has come, he [Jesus] said. 'The kingdom of God has come near. <u>Repent and believe the good news!</u>'"* (Mk. 1:15).

One of the most important factors in changing your life is *repentance*. The repentance called for throughout the Bible is a personal, sincere, and complete surrender to God. It includes remorse and regret, but it is more than that. When you repent, you make a complete change in direction toward God. You stop doing whatever sin you committed before and make a 180-degree about-face. *Have you had that moment when you made a complete and sincere surrender to God?*

It is crucial to leave whatever past you came from and never go back. You will know you have made the change as you recover because you won't want to return to how you once were. You will be tempted as I was when I went to Pappadeaux's during my lunch hour. The only seat open was next to the draft beer. That voice from the past whispered, "No one will know." I had to pray because I knew I needed to detox from 30 years of drinking. God gave me the grace I needed to order a club soda with lime as I devoured the lunch special of Texas Redfish Pontchartrain. I felt proud to tell Irma I even sat across from the draft beer and did not have one.

Asking God for forgiveness is also part of the transformation you are attempting to make. You must be specific about what you did without any excuses as to what made you sin. You must take personal responsibility as God's forgiveness will not come without the admission of guilt. You must also have a feeling of remorse for your action. Tell God exactly what you did, even though He already knows it. Then you must have the faith that God has forgiven you as far as the east is from the west. Satan will try to remind you that you are not good enough and you will fail again. You do not have to keep asking God for forgiveness or staying stuck in the quicksand called guilt.

One of my favorite uncles (RIP) expressed guilt to me during our last conversation. He told me he did not know if he would get to Heaven because of the terrible things he did as an adolescent. At that time, I did not know how to teach him about God's forgiveness. Please keep in mind, as long as you have breath, there is time for forgiveness. Unlike us, God never gives up on a person. Remember the story of the thief who was crucified next to Jesus, when this thief asked Jesus to include him when Jesus went into His Kingdom. *"Jesus answered him, I tell you the truth, today you will be with me in paradise"* (Lk. 23:43).

That same Jesus who died on the cross healed my heart and saved me from physical and spiritual death. He thought of each one of us as He sacrificed himself on the Cross.

## Given a Life Sentence

*"Above all else, guard your heart, for everything you do flows from it"* (Prov. 4:23).

68

It is like a modified oxymoron when you receive a life sentence as your punishment. A life sentence is a prison term that typically lasts for one's lifetime. *Isn't that really a death sentence?*

Let's explore the term "life sentence" in both the physical and spiritual realm. In 2013, I was living a death sentence as my heart was in poor condition. Physically I could do no strenuous work, get too emotional, or forget to take my medication. I was taking a stroll toward the grave and about to take a dirt nap.

Exhaustion and worry consumed me with thoughts of when a stroke would hit or my heart would suddenly stop. Every time my irregular heartbeat got stuck on full steam ahead, my chances of suffering a stroke increased dramatically. This required visits to the ER to get my heart rate back to normal rhythm. I asked my cardiologist, "How fast of a heart rate is too fast?" and "How long of a period of an increased heart rate is too long?" His response was, "As long as you can take it!" I told him I cannot live this way. He informed me of a new procedure called an ablation, which could only be performed by a medical doctor specialized in cardiac electrophysiology. I'm pleased to report I recently visited Dr. Kristopher Heinzman on my annual visit, and he said my heart is still functioning perfectly. Dr. Heinzman is recognized as one of the best physicians for this type of surgery. He gave me verbal permission to mention him in this book.

Long story short, here's a fast-forward from *Broken Walk: Searching for Wisdom* to the recovery room:

After a three-hour heart ablation, I woke up in recovery with 10–12 other patients who had just come out of surgery. My mind went into "test mode" for determining if I had suffered a stroke. I knew if I extended my tongue out and it remained limp or hanging to one side, I had failed the test. This would mean I was stroked out. I stuck out my tongue and moved it from right to left. As my tongue slid into my mouth, I smiled and thanked God out loud. A nurse said, "He's not supposed to be awake yet!" My next test was to perform a memory check conducted by Dr. Roo (me). This self-test was to check my brain as I excavated in the caverns of my memory. As I remembered Christmas in 1958, I saw my cousin Mariam receiving a toy monkey with cymbals, and I shouted, "Yes!" As I raised my right arm in praise, a nurse reprimanded me and told me to "be still!" Hmmm—I've heard those words before. God had brought me back from the dead.

On the physical side, I am feeling great more than 7 years after the ablation. I occasionally do dumb things such as going into a room in the house and not remembering why. LOL. My long-term memory is top-notch but my short-term memory is (pause)...sorry, I forgot what I was writing.

On the spiritual side, I am no longer a walking, clueless zombie.

On November 13, 1999, my life changed! I was given an eternal life sentence by Jesus Christ. I am a new creation and now, *"I have been crucified with Christ and I no longer live, but Christ lives in me"* (Gal. 2:20). So read this part closely: if I no longer live, does that mean I received a death sentence? *Absolutely not!* It is another modified oxymoron in the spiritual realm as I have been given life abundantly. I have never had more freedom! Now I pray that as a "prisoner for the Lord," (Ephes. 4:1) I am able to live a life worthy of the calling I have received. Thank you, Jesus!

When I sincerely asked Jesus to come into my heart on that crisp November morning, my change was instant. Immediately, a wave of warmth covered me from head to toe, and electricity danced in my veins. My lungs got unclogged as I breathed in life. A 100-pound weight was taken off my shoulders.

I have wondered if a heart physically changes when you receive salvation. The following is taken in part from *Broken Walk: Searching for Wisdom*.

If my heart could talk, would it tell you my addiction to alcohol is gone? Would feelings of anger, resentment, hatred, jealousy, plotting revenge, unforgiveness, loneliness, and selfishness no longer be there?

Does a heart make a noise when it changes? Is there a sound when it transforms from stone to freshly plowed ground? Does the blood flow sound like a babbling brook? Would the sound you hear resemble a giggle from a young child? Does a heart sing when your soul is forgiven? Is there a sweet sound like a bird's song as it awaits the sunrise? Perhaps the sound is like the delicate ping from the triangle during a symphony. Once you get set free, your heart will never be the same. My heart now sings perpetual tunes without words and will never stop praising.

Jesus gave me a life sentence when he healed my heart, so now I will spend the rest of my life in solitary confinement serving Him only. *"As a prisoner for the Lord, then, I urge you to live a life worthy of the calling you have received. Be completely humble and gentle; bearing with one another in love. Make every effort to keep the unity of the Spirit through the bond of peace. There is one body and one Spirit, just as you were called to one hope when you were called; one Lord, one Faith, one baptism; one God and Father of all, who is over all and through all and in all"* (Ephes. 4:1–6).

## Are You Ready to Receive Your Life Sentence?

Our problem is we are born with a heart issue that causes us to sin on a regular basis. In other words, the heart of the problem is the problem of the human heart. A wicked heart in a wicked person will not change. The problem is sin, the answer is Jesus. We try not to sin, but we still do. The sinful nature is selfish, self-centered, self-promoting, and self-preserving. Each of us was born into the world with this nature, but Jesus was born into this world to take it away.

## The Living Water

There is a wonderful story in the book of John Chapter 4 that tells of Jesus talking with a Samaritan woman. At that time, this was taboo because Jews did not associate with Samaritans. In their conversation Jesus asks her for a drink of water. He then offers her living water and then reveals He is the Messiah. The woman went into town to tell others about her encounter with the Lord. Subsequently many Samaritans from that town believed in Jesus because of the woman's testimony.

When we meet and form a personal relationship with Jesus, we can continuously draw joy from the well of salvation. The joy of the Lord is our strength. We must immerse ourselves regularly in His Living Water so we will never be thirsty again. Flood the reservoir of your mind and soul to extinguish any fiery darts or flaming arrows from the enemy. We are in a struggle against spiritual forces of evil. *"Therefore, put on the full armor of God so that when the day of evil comes, you will be able to hold your ground"* (Ephes. 6:13). Along with this armor, your feet will be fitted with readiness that comes from the gospel of peace so you can stand your ground. Keep a spiritual basin full of Living Water to wash away any filth that comes from the darkness of the world.

Flashback moment: when we were at our coldest and darkest moments in February 2021 with no power, heat, or water in our power outage, we began to worry. Our normal water supply was gone, and we thought the pipes were frozen. We prayed, and God provided an answer. We gathered and melted snow to flush down our worries, waste, and stench. The solution came from God because this former desert dweller from south of the tracks had no clue what to do next. *"If you believe, you will receive whatever you ask for in prayer"* (Mk. 11:23).

## Making the Right Decision

The purpose of this first part of the book is to *get you ready* to go to Heaven. It all begins by making the decision to focus on the eternal. It comes with an unshakable faith that makes you turn over control of your life to God. You must be all in with your commitment! The decision you make will be forever. Be ready for the remainder of your earthly life by turning control over to God. If you take care of what your soul needs now, God will take care of your soul for eternity.

The sparkle of earthly things are not always as they appear. Make good decisions and not hasty ones. Quick choices without prayer can sometimes come with a lifetime of regret or punishment. There are many individuals who are not incarcerated only because they got lucky and did not get caught.

*"Trust in the Lord with all your heart and lean not on your own understanding; in all your ways acknowledge Him, and He will make your paths straight"* (Prov. 3:5–6).

This doesn't guarantee that life will get easier because there will always be the temptation of sin laying at our doorstep. The essence of deception sometimes happens so slowly that when you realize it is wrong, you have already fallen deep into the trap of sin. Whenever you get off the purpose of what God has designated for your life, the path becomes crooked and rugged.

Thank God for the gifts of grace and mercy. *Grace* is part of the unmerited favor that God gave to humanity by sending Jesus to die on a cross, thus making a way to provide atonement for our sins. There is also *mercy* that God has shown us as we could never do enough to attain admission into Heaven by our acts alone. Sometimes these two attributes are used interchangeably, but grace and mercy differ in many ways.

In a nutshell, grace is a gift we don't deserve, while mercy is not getting the punishment we deserve. Grace is not asked for, but it is freely given. Mercy is an act to relieve someone from their suffering.

We have some classic stories of men and women throughout the Bible who God used to fulfill His Purpose. He showered them with mercy and grace.

The teenage Mary was full of *grace* and had the greatest honor of giving birth to our Savior.

Noah was a drunk who received God's *mercy* and later he had the faith to build an ark.

Abram was a liar and told Sara to say she was his sister so the Pharaoh would have *mercy* and not kill them. Abraham later received the promise of God's grace: *"I will make your offspring like the dust of the earth, so if anyone can count the dust, then your offspring could be counted"* (Gen. 13:16).

Then there's the story of David, the shepherd boy, giant killer, who became king. He was a man after God's own heart. He committed adultery and arranged a murder. God was *merciful* to him.

Saul, who became Paul, was a zealot in his pursuit to kill Christians, but God showed him complete *mercy*. After Saul met the Lord on his way to Damascus, he made a complete change and became an avid follower of the Way. He had to suffer many hardships as a result. 2 Corinthians 11:23–28 tell us what Paul had to endure – *". . . in labors more abundant, in stripes above measure, in prisons more frequently, in deaths often. From the Jews five times I received forty stripes minus one. Three times I was beaten with rods; once I was stoned; three times I was shipwrecked; a night and a day I have been in the deep; in jour-neys often, in perils of waters, in perils of robbers, in perils of my own countrymen, in perils of the Gentiles, in perils in the city, in perils in the wilderness, in perils in the sea, in perils among false brethren; in weariness and toil, in sleeplessness often, in hunger and thirst, in fastings often, in cold and nakedness."* Paul did this for the glory of God alone. We must follow Paul's example to show God we are fully committed as we *get ready* to go to Heaven.

I bring up these biblical examples to remind us God never changes and we are all recipients of God's grace and mercy as well. Despite our sinning repeatedly, He continues to show us His kindness and compassion. He even sent His only Son so all of us can be saved — this is an act of *grace* that we do not deserve.

My simple Simon explanation of grace and mercy is put this way:

Suppose I caught someone inside my house in a robbery attempt, and Irma was able to tie him up like a mummy. (She is a seamstress after all.) The robber apologizes to us and tells how he was desperate and low on cash. Even though he is subdued and bound, we decide to pardon the robber and let the matter go without calling the police — that's mercy (also, dumb). If we then decided to give this robber some food and money to help him through his period of desperation — that's grace. (I can't see myself doing that.) Hope this helps in distinguishing the difference of the two Godly gifts of grace and mercy given to us, His children.

## Let's Get Personal

Let me make this very personal and real — this book is about showing you how to *get ready* to go to Heaven and what to do while we *get set* to go. If you were to die tonight, do you know without any doubt whatsoever that you would go to Heaven? This is too important to say, "I think so" or "I hope so." If you're wrong, you're going to be wrong and suffering for a long, long time.

What we all need is solid ground on which to stand. That solid ground is found in the death and resurrection of Jesus Christ. Our entire hope of Heaven is wrapped up in what Jesus did when He died on the cross for the sins of the world and rose from the dead on Resurrection Sunday morning. He is the Lamb, the sacrifice of God, who takes away the sin of the world.

One of my favorite lyrics[8] in a song goes like this:

*My hope is built on nothing less*
*Than Jesus's blood and righteousness;*

*I dare not trust the sweetest frame,*
*But wholly lean on Jesus's name.*
*On Christ the solid rock I stand;*
*All other ground is sinking sand;*
*All other ground is sinking sand.*

That says it all. If you want to go to Heaven, you must base your hope on the solid rock of Jesus's blood and righteousness. *Are you standing on the Rock right now? Are you putting all your trust in Jesus?*

No one goes to Heaven by serendipity. Heaven is God's *prepared* place for *prepared* people. We prepare on earth to go Heaven to the place God has already prepared for us. Most people believe in Heaven, and most people think they are going there. But are they truly on their *golden walk*? Do they think they are going to Heaven because they are more good than bad? Are they praying to a statue or saint rather than Jesus? Too many, I fear, are standing on sinking sand and do not even know it.

What is your way to get to heaven? There is only One Way, through Jesus Christ. I'm all in with my complete trust in Jesus alone. If He can't take me to Heaven, *then I'm not going there.* What about you? When the dark of night comes, the lights go out, and the waters of death and nightmares of doubt swirl around you, what will happen to you then? Will you be doubtful and full of fear? Will the fear of death cause you to have ungodly visions or anxiety? If you know Jesus, you have nothing to fear. *Put your trust in Jesus; run to the Cross and surrender.* Stand with your full weight on the Solid Rock of our salvation. May God help you to trust in Jesus Christ and Him alone for your salvation. And may God grant that we will all meet one day in Heaven. Then we will be safe at home at last.

No one will go to Heaven except by the grace of God and through the merits of the blood of Jesus Christ. If a man says no to Jesus, he has no hope of Heaven.

I'll be there. What about you?

Here are nine steps to Heaven; part of your *golden walk* is to look up the scriptures.

1. God's part: God sent His Son (Jn. 3:16; 1 Jn. 4:10)

2. Jesus's part: Jesus shed His Blood (Ephes. 1:7; 1 Pet. 1:19)

3. The Holy Spirit's part: the Word revealed through the Holy Spirit (Jn. 16:13)

4. Our part: faith comes from hearing (Rom. 10:17; Jn. 6: 44–45)

5. Our part: we must believe (Rom. 10:9–10, 13; Jn. 8:24)

6. Our part: we must repent of sins (Acts 2:38, 17:30)

7. Our part: we must confess and proclaim (Rom. 10:9–10; Acts 8:37)

8. Our part: baptism into Christ (Mk. 16:16; 1 Pet. 3:21)

9. Our part: remain faithful (Col. 1:21–23; Rev. 2:10)

This chapter and Part 1 of the book finishes by leaving you with a yarn about making the wrong decision from my late brother-in-law Danny Mendoza, who is rejoicing in paradise.

A man after dying finds himself in the chambers of hell accompanied by Lucifer himself. The always clever host asks the man to make a choice of three scenarios that will be the man's new life for eternity.

- In the first choice, the devil shows the man a room in which a lost soul is sitting on a chair and drinking coffee in rotting sewage that reaches up to his ankles.

- The second option is a room where there's a man standing in toxic feces up to his waistline.

- In the third chamber was someone standing in the grossest human waste that goes all the way up to his chin.

The devil asks the man, "Which one do you choose? Remember, this is irrevocable and it is for eternity!

The condemned man quickly, responds, "I'll take the first choice!"

Satan then places the man in the first scenario. The man looks around and quickly remarks, "Hey! Where's my chair and coffee?"

Satan laughs in a resounding echo and says, "The guy in the first room was on coffee break, it is now time for you to stand on your head! The laughter continues as Satan walks away.

**Golden Step #6: Choose to follow Jesus *today*; no one reaches Heaven except through Him.**

# PART TWO – GET SET

## CHAPTER 7

# GIVE THANKS

*"Give thanks in all circumstances; for this is God's will for you in Christ Jesus"* (1 Thess. 5:18).

Now that you have read Part One of this book ("Get Ready"), I pray that you have formed a personal relationship with Christ. If not, keep reading.

When I was a young boy, we used to swim in the irrigation canals in Phoenix, Arizona. Sometimes the water moved swiftly, and it was difficult to get out of the canal without assistance. The help came from a rope that was tied across the fast-moving water. It felt great and reassuring to grab the rope and then being able to pull yourself out. My father was usually at the end making sure my siblings, cousins, and I got out safely. If you missed the rope, Yikes! I never did, so here I am writing about it.

Think of my memory in the canal representing the journey of life. It can move you aimlessly, bobbing you up and down as you keep your head above water. There were times when our cutoff pants would be torn on the seat from the friction. You could also get cuts from cracks in the cement when you went under a small bridge that caused the water to go faster and it was more slippery. The rope (lifeline) represents

Jesus. At some point in our journey, we must grab ahold of Him so we can make it into the security of our Father, represented by my earthly father.

Now is a good time to grab the lifeline as Jesus is standing at the entrance to your heart and wants to come in. *"Behold, I stand at the door and knock. If anyone hears my voice and opens the door, I will come in <u>to</u> him and dine with him and he with Me"* (Rev. 3:20). Those words are His words, His promise. Grab the lifeline — and you will be full of gratitude.

*"Though you do not see Him, yet believing, you rejoice with joy inexpressible and full of glory, receiving the end of your faith — the salvation of your soul"* (1 Pet. 1:8–9).

## It All Begins with an Attitude of Gratitude!

Being joyful isn't what makes you grateful; being grateful is what makes you joyful! You need to think about your life and then live daily when you see miracles in life every day. S.M.I.L.E. — even when you don't feel like it. If you see someone without a smile, give yours away. Even if they don't smile back, it will make them wonder why you are always smiling, and you can tell them something like, "Because Jesus *reigns* in my heart; therefore, His Love *rains* from my heart in the form of a smile."

Write down what you are thankful for. Here is my short list. I am keeping it simple because that's who I am; I thought about four areas of life:

- **God** — the great *I AM.* Because of Him, *I am* no longer insecure; *I am* God-secure. *I am* no longer afraid to die but instead *I am* ready to fly. Be it by Uppertaker or undertaker.

- **Family**—Having people around me that genuinely love me unconditionally and accept me with all my imperfections and corny way of expressing myself.

- **Health**—Thank you, Jesus, as my heart has been made new in the physical and the spiritual. In 2013, an ablation fixed the physical irregularities. My spiritual heart is at peace, full of His Love. It sings a continuous song that has its unique lyrics of praise.

- **Work**—Even though I am retired, my job is now to write about His Goodness. Because of this, I am able to give away whatever proceeds I receive from book sales. What a blessing!

*"What a wretched man I am! Who will rescue me from this body of death?"* (Rom. 7:24). Thanks be to God, the great I AM—my salvation is from His gift to us, Jesus Christ, our Lord.

Here's an untitled short poem I found in my study Bible, which I wrote probably around 2004 (at that point, I was serving as the postmaster in Odessa, Texas):

Thank you, Lord, for that extra pinch of sleep
It keeps me seasoned before that alarm clock beep
I peeked at the clock and it glared 3:16
I smiled as I thanked Jesus for waking me up again
As I prayed while I lay there warm and secure
My thoughts filled with gratitude for all you endured
Another day is upon me, and I wonder what it will bring
There will be coffee, my Bible, and some birds to sing
No matter how much mail is at the post office today
My trust is in You to show me how to lead the Way

## Four Buttonholes of Life Represent Who You Are

I like to think there are four areas of what makes up a person. In a simple illustration, these four parts are: physical, spiritual, work, and family. Think about a button with the four holes on it. Each hole is the same size, and when it is sewn onto clothing correctly, the button is secure and stable. During those days when I was assigned to USPS headquarters, the work buttonhole was getting all the thread, while the other three buttonholes received very little thread and were not stable. A person's life must have balance with the right mix of thread being applied to the four buttonholes equally. The way I carried myself during those days in DC would have qualified me to perform in Michael Jackson's "Thriller" video.

Examine these four areas of your life and determine if you need to make some adjustments.

My buttonhole examination came on my weekend trip back to Texas in January 2012. At that time, I was on an assignment at USPS headquarters in Washington, DC. Irma and I were apart physically, and I came home every third weekend. Our time away from each other was not good for our relationship. I remember asking Irma to fix a loose button on my heavy winter coat. She fixed it for me as if she were a surgeon carefully putting stitches on a patient after open heart surgery. I promised her things would improve, but she responded that those were just words. I headed back to Washington with my head hung low. I was now a walking zombie—just burning daylight in a dark time. I somehow knew deep inside of me that if I fixed the spiritual, God would take care of the rest.

**Even Now God**

My blessing came when I returned to Washington, DC, and connected with National Community Church led by Pastor Mark Batterson. There are several locations in this remarkable church around the DC Metro area. I came across one by fluke but lost concentration when the service consisted of the Pastor's message on a live telecast. I had no intention of returning, but on the way out, I was given a book he had written. His book, entitled *The Circle Maker*,[9] brought me back from those dark days and lonely nights. I soon found the main congregation for Sunday service and joined a men's group near Ebenezer's Coffee House. It was like drinking refreshing, Living Water that went directly into my parched soul. It is an incredible blessing to join in worship with 30+ men while singing songs such as *"How Great Thou Art"* and *"Amazing Grace."* My loneliness subsided as I became more balanced. Soon I was able to share with Irma some of what I had learned. One of the most powerful lessons was the message about Even Now God.

This story is about Jesus's conversation with Lazarus's sister Martha when He arrived at Bethany. His friend Lazarus had been dead and buried for four days. "Lord," Martha said to Jesus, "if you had been here, my brother would not have died. But I know that <u>even now God</u> will give you whatever you ask" (Jn. 11:21–22). Irma was skeptical when I told her that our *even now God* could restore our severed relationship.

The days seemed to speed by like a cheetah driving a Chevy, and even though our conversations were improving, it was now February. I prayed to receive a Valentine from Irma, and in the final minutes just before midnight on February 14, 2012, I received an e-Valentine. She said it was the one she intended to give me in 2011. I went to work the next morning with renewed hope only to later hear the worst news that has ever trampled into my ears. Irma called me and asked me to get to a location where I could sit down. After I locked myself in a small conference room, she let me know her mother had died in a single car accident. This news made my knees wobble, and I almost threw up. As she gave me other details, it felt like my heart and soul were no longer a part of me. I had to get off the phone to compose myself as I was wailing out loud within the walls of USPS headquarters. After several minutes, my focus went back to Irma, and I knew I had to provide her with empathy, support, and compassion. The trip back to Texas was difficult, and I will always be indebted to Steve and my daughter-in-law Misti for taking care of me and Irma during this most difficult time in my life.

After a few weeks, Irma and I ran away and reconciled at a stay in Runaway Bay near Fort Worth. We were there for a week and went into every detail of what caused us to split apart. There were times when we shed tears from laughing and at other times, felt the hot waterworks turned on by anger. There were three instances at this reconciliation station that we cannot explain. The first one came when we both saw a flesh bubble that rose on the left side of her bosom. It alarmed both of us as it looked like her heart was pushing in an attempt to escape from her body. After we prayed, we felt a sense of peace and concluded Irma was given a new heart. This heart could now accept and transfuse love back to my heart. We were reconnected and overjoyed with our decision to get back together.

The next unexplainable incident happened as we were packing prior to leaving. As we removed clothing from the small closet, we both saw electricity bouncing for several seconds like volts in a crystal ball. We were surprised and had to pray so we would not be spooked by this unusual display of electrical energy. The last occurrence came when we were in our rented vehicle heading east toward Ft. Worth. I was driving, and we were content driving at the posted 70 miles per hour speed limit. All the sudden, all the windows inside the vehicle became fogged up, and we could not see anything past any window. I quickly turned on the flashers as Irma furiously wiped at this attack to no avail. I opened my driver side window and commanded this presence to leave our vehicle in the name of Jesus. I remember saying, "You don't scare me, you don't even have a birth certificate!" I was referring to Lucifer himself. The windows cleared even faster than when it attached itself to the windows. I had to pull over, and we talked about the future ahead of us before continuing our journey together in life.

She joined me in Washington, DC, and we made vows to each other under the cherry blossoms in March 2012 to never separate again. The remaining time in DC was a difficult period for her as she was dealing with the grief of losing her mother. I distracted her with a couple of trips to Puerto Rico where we zip-lined through El Yunque jungle and we also later drove to Niagara Falls.

Since that dark period in our marriage, God has taken care of us more than you will ever know! Because of this, *I am* forever grateful.

Along this journey in my life, I have met many individuals that have influenced me positively. The common characteristic they possess is gratitude mixed with faith.

## Pizza the Hutt

The first person I want to present was a young man that was born with a physical deformity His head was a normal size, but his body did not develop. He had miniature arms and legs, and he was confined to a wheelchair. He was able to scoot around on the ground quickly. At full height, he stood about two and a half feet tall. This teenaged young man was part of a youth group attending a Christian conference that I chaperoned during an overnight outing. He was incredible as he made up for his handicap with his superior intellect and positive attitude.

My nickname for him was Pizza the Hutt, his self-proclaimed name like the Star Wars character called Jabba the Hutt. He loved having a reason to go down the hallway of the hotel room and knock on the door of the hotel room where a group of young ladies from our group were staying. He found various ways to get their attention. It was incredible to see him dance on his wheelchair, and he made sound effects like he was driving a car. On one occasion, when we made a purchase from Pizza Hut, he asked me to go with him to deliver a pizza to his female friends. He had me set the box of pizza on the floor near their doorway and then ring their doorbell. He stood there with the pizza and announced, "Hello, I'm Pizza the Hutt!" The girls erupted in laughter and devoured the pizza in a matter of minutes.

He loved roughhousing with the boys in our group and begged me to allow him to wrestle on the king-size bed. He was full of joy as he received atomic bombs and body slams. He was rambunctious, and some of the boys let him pin them. He and I developed a way to tease each other. When he sat next to me on a chair to eat a meal, he would pretend like he was losing his balance to keep me on edge.

Once I realized this was intentional, I moved his plate away from him where he could not reach it with his diminutive arms. Before going to sleep, he entertained us with voice impersonations and jokes. He occasionally turned serious like when he thanked me for allowing him to visit the girls and being able to wrestle. The last time I saw him was when I dropped him off at the church, and he grabbed on to my ankle like a garrapata (tick) and playfully yelled, "Daddy, daddy, don't leave!" He enjoyed that I took a few steps with him attached to my leg.

Pizza the Hutt had more life than any of the other boys even with his limitations. He made the most of all his abilities and left his footsteps in my memory on how to be grateful.

## Stinky Beak

Ever since he entered my life back in 1962, my brother Big Ern has always had an exceptional attitude. He was born with Down Syndrome, and his development was stymied with a prognosis of leukemia when he was a baby. He did not learn to walk until he was five. The doctors told my parents he was probably not going to make it, so they prayed until something happened (**PUSH**) with other prayer warriors from Our Lady of Fatima Church. Next, the medical experts said he would only live until his teens; Ernie is still kicking at age 58. Although he was legally blind most of his life, he managed to take the city bus from south Phoenix (with a transfer downtown) by himself to his sheltered workshop.

He is an avid sports fan and is aggressively loyal if you talk about his team. The same goes if you disrespect Michael or Janet Jackson. He enjoys dancing, especially when he has an audience. One of my favorite memories of him was when he came home from where he worked and told me he got into a fight. He told me he won and demonstrated how he used the "Ali shuffle" to defeat his opponent. When I asked him if he had been hit, he laughed and said the other guy was blind. I told him, "I can't believe you beat up a blind guy!" He said the guy kept bugging him every day, and he finally got tired of it. He said, "He never saw my punches coming!"

Ernie has brought a lifetime of joy to our family and is a practical joker. He loves to scare me as he hides at various spots and waits for me to walk by. He also enjoys telling me that he is a vampire and he is going to drink my blood. Sometimes when I talk to him on the phone, a random "blood" remark will sneak in from the blue. When I question it, he always denies saying it.

My father told me he was once with him at Walmart and Ernie grabbed a pair of large woman panties and put them near his (my father's) rear to measure if their size was a good fit. Big Ern had snuck up on my father and some people in the store were chuckling to see him do this.

I'm thankful that I was able to spend a Saturday morning with him recently. We had a wonderful morning as we ate the breakfast of champions. Two of my friends, Rick Quiroz Sr., and Robert Robles (both aspiring authors) joined us. Big Ern was thrilled to be one of the guys. Our morning ended with a haircut and a shave. He would not let me trim his fingernails even though they were screeching desperately to be cut.

Eating the breakfast of champions.

## Worship Leaders

I'm always amazed at the way praise and worship leaders are so upbeat and able to get into the moment even when they might be having personal issues going on. What's their secret? They know that their singing can bring in the presence of God. This leads to the healing of the hurting. One of my close friends who has been in ministry (Christian songwriting and singing) for almost 50 years told me he loves to hear the stories of how a song he wrote touches someone. That is what makes it all worth it. His name is Joel Perales. He and his wife, Rose, have been in ministry since the day after they married; in June 2021 they celebrated their 50th anniversary.

Brother Joel had a rough year in 2020 as three brothers and one sister died throughout the year. He and Rose never lost focus on their ministry during these times of sorrow. They continued to worship regularly through their Perales Ministry Hour online as churches were closed and people were advised to stay home because of COVID-19. They celebrated their one-year anniversary of this ministry on March 20, 2021. It was awesome to see their home full of an abundance of gifts from listeners. Most importantly, they were surrounded by their children and their spouses, along with all their grandchildren. Their gratitude burst through the social media of Facebook as they once again ushered us into His Courts with praise. God bless the Perales Family with continued strength until we all celebrate in that angelic choir, forevermore. With a heart full of gratitude, we thank you for letting Irma and I join you online and at your home in Nashville recently. *True worshipers never leave church; they carry it with them, along with others, all the way into Heaven.*

## Darkest Hour

Even in my darkest hour, through my sorrow and the pain, I will sing and be grateful. My turning point came at the Los Angeles Dream Center while on a short term mission trip. After our day at skid row in downtown LA, that night, I was alone in the dark in my bunk bed. Earlier in the day, God showed me examples of *humility* and *purpose* through a home-less man. I prayed with gratitude as I finally understood my purpose for the remainder of my life. For this I am forever grateful. I will do all I can to bring glory to God alone through writing. (More on this in Chapter 12)

With my hero Tommy Barnett at the Phoenix Dream City Church

I wrote the poem below to describe some of my life issues that knocked me down for a season. After I refocused, I came back stronger with increased strength and gratitude. If you need more explanation on the poem, send me a message at rubengee820@gmail.com. The poem was written after I had taken a picture in Bandera, Texas, with me surrounded by the remains of a burned-out, hollow tree. This picture was taken shortly after attending a "Cowboy Church" service. I remember at the service, asking for prayer because I needed peace in the midst of chaos. God blessed me with peace that day and restored my joy. I will always be grateful for the ultimate sacrifice Jesus paid for me. I hope you like this poem.

## Rise Up!

No matter how many times life knocks you down
Get up with more *ganas*, and get rid of that frown

Setbacks are a bump on the journey that will not last
As long as you learn and make them a thing of the past

Life issues grab you and pull you deep into the ground
Making you stuck in your darkness, with no one around

Only you really know the innermost thoughts in your head
You hear it over and over — even words that were not said

Want More and Selfish were right next to me
Good character is corrupted by bad company

Alcohol and ambition tried to make an ash out of Gee
But like the phoenix from ashes, he stepped out of that tree

Stronger than ever, I am able to tell my story
Now my life is not about me, it's all for His glory

Jesus pulled me out of the darkness and into His light
Making it easy to walk because His Word is so bright

The best choice I made was a life commitment to Him
Now I have love, peace, and joy while wearing my brim

**Rise up** and ask Him to show you the Way
He'll carry you forward into Peace on your final day.

*"Arise, shine, for your light has come,*
*and the glory of the LORD rises upon you"* (Isa. 60:1).

**Golden Step #7: Be grateful and S.M.I.L.E. — See Miracles
In Life Everyday.**

# CHAPTER 8

## SAME POWER

*"The <u>same power</u> that raised Christ from the dead is living in you"* (Rom. 8:11).

Now that we are followers of Christ's part of the inheritance, we receive the *same* great *power* that rose Jesus from the dead. This gives me immense hope and reassurance to go forward with the plan God has for me for the remainder of my life. I pray for wisdom daily because of the promise found in James 1:5: "If any of you lacks wisdom, you should ask God who gives generously to all without finding fault, and it will be given to you." God is also kind enough to equip us with spiritual gifts when we have our new life in Christ. "But each of you has your own gift from God; one has this gift, another has that" (1 Cor. 7:7). It is important for us to recognize our gift and use it. This spiritual gift is not so much to help us as individuals but to help others in the Body of Christ to increase our faith and glorify God.

One of the spiritual gifts I received is the *gift of healing*. It happened at nighttime on the day I had earlier received salvation. *Here's an excerpt from Barrio Walk: Stepping into Wisdom.*

Back then, I lived in Little Rock, and it was a long drive home from Fort Worth where my future wife lived. That night

I got home exhausted from my salvation experience and the five-and-a-half-hour drive. I went straight to bed, and as I lay down, it felt like I was coming down with the flu; my dry throat was closing faster than a snapping turtle. Under the covers I was freezing and had the chills. As I shivered, I prayed to God to remove whatever illness was invading my body. This was one of my first prayers other than the Our Father or Hail Mary. God in His goodness and mercy answered me. It felt like something physically wiped my throat with a soft but firm touch. Immediately, there was a feeling again, the wave of warmth, peace, and love that covered me from head to toe, and I began to sweat. It was awesome to feel the healing hand of God! The new creation in Christ fell asleep and woke up refreshed without any sign of illness. "Therefore, if anyone is in Christ, the new creation has come: The old has gone, the new is here" (2 Cor. 5:17).

No matter what you are going through, the healing hand of God can heal you too. He loves you and can take away anything you may be suffering from with one touch. It could be illness, loneliness, shame, guilt, or depression. He can take it away immediately.

God loves us more than we love ourselves. He has promised to give us the desires of our heart. "Take delight in the Lord, and He will give you the desires of your heart" (Ps. 37:4). He knows what we need before we even ask. "Ask and it shall be given to you; seek and you will find; knock and the door will be opened for you" (Matt. 7:7).

*What if* right now in Heaven there is a warehouse full of miracles waiting to happen? In one storage room there may be new hearts, in another thousands of livers or pancreas. *What if* we don't receive because we don't ask?

## All about Him and There Must Be Belief

One of my former co-workers likes to call me the Extension Cord. This nickname is from an explanation I use to connect to that same power that raised Jesus from the dead. He first asked me to pray for his son who was having seizures that could not be explained in a perfectly healthy teenager. His son received a healing touch from our Lord and has not had another seizure since the initial prayer. The same friend recently sent me an email and asked me to call his aunt who was having some medical issues. When I called her, she told me she was worried about a lump because she had already had two mammograms that showed a growth. After our praying, Jesus took away the lump, and it was no longer detected on the third examination, which was done by ultrasound. Praise the Lord! Jesus is the same yesterday, today, and forever. He still performs miracles every day!

Our Bible is a miracle digest. Creation was a miracle— God spoke into a handful of dirt, and man became a living soul. When God divided the Red Sea, it was a miraculous crossing for Moses and three million Israelites so they could escape the pharaoh. Three Hebrew young men were thrown into a fiery furnace when they refused to bow down to the king's image, and a fourth person showing up was a mighty phenomenon. When mankind really needed God the most, He does not send someone, He shows up in a manger. The virgin birth was a miracle; if Jesus was not born through a virgin, then He is not the Son of God. It would make our gospel a farce and our faith a fraud.

His first miracle of changing water into wine was just the start, and it was impressive. During that first miracle he turned water inside six stone jars into wine instantly. Each of the water jars held 20 to 30 gallons of water so that's 120 to

180 gallons of choice wine so the wedding celebration could continue. Jesus performed countless miracles. "If every one of them were written down, I suppose that even the whole world would not have room for the books that would be written" (Jn .21:25). Be reassured, based on God's word, that Jesus is the miracle-born Son of God.

## Spiritual Gifts

The Bible references there are 21 Gifts of the Spirit.[10] Nine of these gifts are mentioned in 1 Corinthians 12 and are known as the "Power Gifts." These gifts increase power and faith to the Church and to the believers. There are also several extra gifts designed to enriching the Church, to shape it up and to fortify it, and add some extra pizzazz to the Church. Some of these gifts are sometimes downplayed but are vital, legitimate gifts. All of them are manifestations of the activity and of the work and person of the Holy Spirit in a tangible form — they are an expression of His character.

The word "gift" would be translated in Greek as "charisma," which gives the idea of spiritual grace, or a spiritual release of power to give glory to God's essence and power. Believers have different gifts — they're intended to display the glory, power, and magnificence of the Lord. He does miraculous things beyond our understanding. The rest of the gifts are designed for the edification of the Church.

The 21 Gifts of the Holy Spirit are:

1.  **Witnessing Power (Acts 1:8)**–Witnessing is telling others about the forgiveness, love, deliverance, empowering, fruitful life ministry, and so forth, that you found in Jesus.

2. **Mutual Encouragement (Rom. 1:11–12)**–Finding strength in the sharing of each other's faith with believers to persevere and grow in the ministry and teachings of Jesus Christ.

3. **Prophesying (Rom. 12:6, 1 Cor. 12:10)**–To prophesy is to foretell or predict the future as guided by the Holy Spirit. It is the ability to make inspired declarations of what is to come.

4. **Serving (Rom. 12:7)** – Serving others is more than just making sure things get done. You must keep your eyes, heart, and schedule open to divine appointments. It means to regularly care for others.

5. **Teaching (Rom. 12:7)** – Teaching, simply put, is to help another understand.

6. **Encouraging (Rom. 12:8)** – The ability to give someone support or confidence that leads to positive hope for future success.

7. **Contributing (Rom. 12:8)** – The act of providing service, our time, and even financially as needed.

8. **Leadership (Rom. 12:8)** – The process of guiding others, maximizing the efforts toward the achievement of a goal.

9. **Showing Mercy (Rom. 12:8)** – A compassionate treatment having a capacity to forgive or show kindness.

10. **Spirit of Unity (Rom. 15:5)** – A blending of minds and personalities that causes a group of individuals to work as a unified group for a common purpose or goal.

11. **Wisdom (1 Cor. 12:8)** – The ability to think and act using knowledge, experience, understanding, common sense, and insight.

12. **Knowledge (1 Cor. 12:8)** – The spiritual gift of knowledge has been defined as the ability to teach the faith. It is given for the specific purpose of communicating divine revelation.

13. **Faith (1 Cor. 12:9)** – The biblical definition of faith is found in Hebrews 11:1. Simply defined, faith is trusting in something you cannot explicitly prove.

14. **Healing (1 Cor. 12:9)** – By the indwelling of the Holy Spirit, some Christians are gifted to heal real suffering in Christ's name (and only by His name, not for our own glory). This gift cannot be taught and is given and can be taken away according to God's will.

15. **Miraculous Power (1 Cor. 12:10)** – Through the Holy Spirit, having the ability to perform powerful miracles, which could include raising the dead and restoring sight, speech, or hearing and the use of limbs to the lame.

16. **Discernment (1 Cor. 12:10)** – In the simplest definition, it is the ability to decide between truth and error, right or wrong.

17. **Tongues (1 Cor. 12:10)** – Granted by the Holy Spirit, it is the ability to speak in another language unbeknownst to them.

18. **Interpretation (1 Cor. 12:10)** – The supernatural ability to understand the tongue language and translate it.

19. **Administration (1 Cor. 12:28)** – This is considered a team gift because it thrives when called upon to organize people to accomplish an objective.

20. **Revelation (Ephes. 1:17)** – It is supernatural wisdom concerning the divine purpose and plan in the mind and will of God. It is granted by the Holy Spirit when it makes known information in the Word of Wisdom, Word of Understanding, and in the discerning of spirits.

21. **Joy (1 Thess. 1:6)** – The Greek word literally means "for the heart, in its deepest place of passion and feelings, to be well." It is the ability to rejoice in the Lord always, regardless of the circumstances.

My prayer is you discover the spiritual gift God has given you and you exercise it to its full potential. *Stir up in us, Lord, our spiritual gifts to glorify you and to increase our faith.*

Suggesting that a person can just pick and choose a spiritual gift not given to him or her by God can be compared to a child finding and playing with the unwrapped Christmas gifts in the parents' closet. Because these gifts have not been given to the child (us) yet, it is considered a gift that has not been given. It removes the Giver from the equation. How would this make you feel as a parent?

Spiritual gifts from God are given by His will and are not a mark of worthiness. These gifts of the Spirit, by definition, cannot be earned or claimed before God gives them to us.

**Bonus Note:** Some people think their suffering on earth is punishment they must go through to get to Heaven. God has promised repentant believers will inherit His eternal Kingdom through the saving blood of Jesus. That's why Jesus died for us — period. It is not Jesus plus our suffering that makes us worthy of Heaven. If that were the case, then why did Jesus die?

He said it: "I am the way, the Truth and the Life. No one comes to the Father except through Me" (Jn. 14:6).

Only through Christ, who became a helpless baby while keeping the fullness of God, can we find salvation. He was the gift from God that was rejected by the very ones He was sent to save. It was on that cross when Jesus died that the wrath of God was finally fulfilled. Every sin (past, present, and future) was laid on Him; therefore, because of His horrible death, we get to live now and forevermore. Thank you, Jesus! All glory and honor to the Lamb of God, who takes away the sin of the world.

## What Is Your Spiritual Gift?

Perhaps you have more than one. If you have been blessed by God, use your spiritual gift(s) to glorify God and increase the faith of the Body. Personally, I have received the spiritual gifts of healing and teaching.

As a new believer with the gift of healing, I felt like a superhero with a special power minus the cape. It does not work that way. It's all about faith, I am just an extension cord to the source of that *same power* that comes from God. It is that *same power* that rose Jesus from the grave, and that *same power* is conducted through me by faith. It will not work if the person in need of healing does not have faith. Just like you can't jump-start a disabled car with an unserviceable battery, you cannot expect someone to be healed without their wholehearted belief. Jesus is still in the miracle business; all we must do is ask and believe.

There is really no formula that will activate the healing power of God because it does not belong to you. There is a better chance of God's healing touch by being in sync with our Creator.

- First, let go of control and put all your trust in God. It's not an easy thing to do but when you do, it is complete freedom. Pretending you are in control can wear you out.

- Second, align your manner of living to the will of the Father. This gives you a better chance of receiving access to his mighty strength—that *same power* that rose Jesus from the grave.

- Third, invoke the promises in the scriptures. God does not lie, Jesus is the same, yesterday, today, and forever. Ask for a miracle to increase our faith and show us His glory. We have the power of the Holy Spirit living in us. Give thanks in advance to increase our faith through the healing for the glory of God alone. Soli Deo Gloria!

My other gift is teaching. It was the desire of my heart to become an elementary school teacher, but the pay difference that came from the USPS quickly trumped my longing to teach. I love to dig into the Bible and put into simple explanation what God has given us in His love letter. Here is a short version of a lesson that I put together after going on a fishing trip with a couple of friends of 20 years, Lee and Harvey.

We went on a two-day fishing excursion on Lee's new boat named "Fishers of Men." This was a beautiful pontoon boat with lots of bells and whistles.

On our first day we did not catch any fish but had a wonderful time exploring the lake while Lee tested out his new toy. The next day, Lee and Harvey got into several discussions on how to catch fish. Meanwhile, I sat near the back of the boat and caught three largemouth bass. My secret that I did not reveal to them was to use a tiny frog lure. I bounced it off the large cliff-like rock so it appeared like a tiny frog falling into the water. It worked three times for me! They did not catch any fish, so I teased them by saying, "I felt badly for you, so I caught a fish for each of you!"

When we returned to shore, Irma cheerfully took a picture of the three of us with me holding up three largemouth bass. I was the only one in the picture smiling. Later in the day, after we showered and sat around reminiscing about our excursion, Lee remarked, "I can't believe you caught the first fish on my new boat!" I quickly replied, "Correction, I caught the first three fish on your new boat!" As a result of this comment, I have not been invited to go fishing on Lee's boat again for almost 20 years now. Hmmmm, in all fairness, perhaps that is because we had to move away to my next job assignment and haven't seen them in a *long* time.

Sometime after, I had the opportunity to teach on The Lord's Prayer at New Life Chapel. Pastor Marcos Zuniga allowed me several opportunities to teach the congregation. At this study, I was pleased to see both Lee and Harvey in attendance.

The condensed version of this lesson: I began the study by talking about when the apostles asked Jesus to show them how to pray. "One day Jesus was praying in a certain place. When He finished, one of His disciples said to him, 'Lord, teach us to pray, just as John taught his disciples'" (Lk. 11:1). Jesus responded by teaching them a prayer referred to as the Our Father. (This is one of the first prayers I learned as a young child at Our Lady of Fatima in Phoenix. Irma has taught this prayer to each of our six grandboys when they were young. Samuel, who is four years old, is still working on the memorization of it. Cataleya, our only granddaughter, will learn it next. She will be three years old in July 2022.)

Continuing with the lesson, I said, "Wouldn't it be nice if you were trying to learn how to become a great painter and you walked into the classroom and there was Michelangelo? A picture was then displayed on the screen for all to see of Michelangelo working on the ceiling of the Sistine Chapel. Note: Irma was in control of the PowerPoint presentation and controlled what was projected on the overhead screen for the churchgoers to look at.

I followed by saying, "Let's just say someone was wanting to learn karate and they walked into the classroom, and there is Bruce Lee." A picture of Bruce Lee in a striking pose was displayed on the large screen.

Finally, I said, "Suppose there are two guys named Lee and Harvey (Oswald, another of my fishing friends, was not at this service that day) wanting to learn how to fish and they walked into the classroom, and presto—there I was." Irma quickly displayed the picture with me gleefully holding three largemouth bass as our church family roared with laughter. Lee and Harvey laughed and were just shaking their heads. That's what fishing buddies do to each other.

This teaching was concluded about Jesus being the greatest teacher for someone who is asking to learn how to pray. I managed to get serious and taught a sound lesson on the Lord's Prayer that day.

Oh, and incidentally, at one particular church service, I was standing near Lee, Harvey, and Oswald, in that order. I pointed at each of them and exclaimed, "Lee! Harvey! Oswald! I need to get out of here before there is an assassination!" I don't think an opportunity like this will ever happen again. It was just for a moment. Just for us.

I'm blessed to have my desire to teach now fulfilled and satisfied by writing. My gift and ability to write comes from using a formula I learned along the way. When I begin writing, I ask Jesus to help me as I pray for wisdom and creativity. At the end of each chapter, I use the initials SDG, which stand for *Soli Deo Gloria*. It has been used by artists like Johann Sebastian Bach, George Frideric Handel, and Christoph Graupner to signify the work was produced for the sake of praising God. I am blessed this formula is working well for me as my third Christian book will be published within a three-year span. My prayer is the scriptures and stories on *Golden Walk* will encourage you to boldly do things every day to glorify God.

**Golden Step #8: As believers, we have that same power that rose Jesus from the grave.**

# CHAPTER 9

## DO THIS

*"This is my body, which is for you; <u>do this</u> in remembrance of me"* (1 Cor. 11:24).

P art of *getting set* to go to Heaven is obedience. We received a command from our Lord to share bread and wine to commemorate His death. I always look forward to partaking in this ceremonial meal as it connects me more closely to Jesus. This act of obedience makes us remember Your last supper, Your broken body, and Your sin-cleansing blood. The Lord's Supper is about You solely, it focuses us on the reason You came to earth. It is no longer about the Law or Abraham, Isaac, and Jacob. It is remembering You are the Lamb of God — the Only One who takes away the sin of the world. Communion is a sacred form of worship that we should prepare ourselves for before receiving it. We must never take this privilege for granted or lightheartedly.

Here is a short prayer to help prepare you for receiving the Lord's supper.

Lord Jesus, I humbly come before You and ask You to examine my heart today. Reveal to me anything that is not pleasing to You. Show me any secret pride, any uncon-fessed sin, or unforgiveness that may be partially blocking my relationship with You. Thank You for Your extravagant love and grace. I'm grateful because Your death gave me life—abundant life for now, and eternal life forever. I pray this with reverence in Your precious name. Amen.

On the night Jesus was betrayed by Judas, He commanded His apostles to remember Him. *"While they were eating, Jesus took bread, gave thanks and broke it, and gave it to His disciples saying, 'Take this and eat; this is my body.' Then he took the cup, gave thanks and offered it to them, saying, 'Drink from it, all of you. This is my blood of the covenant, which is poured out for many for the forgiveness of sins. I tell you, I will not drink of this fruit of the vine from now on until that day when I drink it anew with you in my Father's kingdom'"* (Matt. 26–29). The account of when Jesus instituted this ordinance of communion is given in Matthew 26:26–29, Mark 14:22-25, Luke 22:19-20, and 1 Corinthians 11:24–26. It is interesting to me to find that the writings found in Matthew 26:30 and Mark 14:26 both finish this account identically, *"When they sung a hymn, they went out to the Mount of Olives."* Jesus and his apostles (minus Judas) proceeded to the Garden of Gethsemane where he was arrested by a great multitude that had swords and clubs.

When I was being prepared for my first communion at Our Lady of Fatima, the nuns would tell us Jesus was inside the small box under the large image of the crucifixion. It was difficult for me to understand how Jesus lived inside the tabernacle on the altar. We were told to be quiet and pray while we were inside the small church. I used to stare at the tabernacle endlessly and tried to figure out how Jesus could fit in that small space.

As I grew older, sadly, I lost my reverence for the sacrament of communion. As an altar boy, prior to mass, we had to get water and wine ready for the upcoming service. Sometimes with another altar boy, we would sneak in a little taste of the wine before the priest arrived. During one of the masses, Ricky, the other altar boy serving with me, tripped and kicked the handheld bells that were rung at various parts of the service. It was spectacular. The clattering bells seemed to tumble for an eternity and the clattering noise filled the whole church. Somehow, I was able to refrain from laughing, and my altar boy partner was super embarrassed. I playfully told Ricky after the service he was going to be arrested for underage drinking.

At the communion service, people came up and kneeled in front of the altar rail to receive communion. While the priest administered communion, I held a golden plate attached with a handle to hold under the person's chin as they received the host from the priest. When certain friends came up, I would sometimes give them a little tap on their throat as their mouth was wide open while having their eyes closed. It was one of those games of composure to see who could be the most *travieso* (mischievous) without laughing or getting caught.

I guess I wouldn't have made it to be able to enter the Holy of Holies back in the Old Testament, when God gave the responsibility to the Levites to do the work associated with the priesthood. Their service came in part with the following instructions: *"But only you and your sons may serve as priests in connection with everything at the altar and inside the curtain. I am giving you the service of priesthood as a gift. Anyone else who comes near the sanctuary is to be put to death"* (Num. 18:7).

There has been much debate over the bread and wine and what it symbolizes. The Roman Catholic Church teaches that Christ is present by transubstantiation. This means that the substance of the bread and wine is miraculously transformed into Christ's body and blood. Other teachings tell us the bread and wine only symbolize His Body and Blood. The most important aspect of both teachings is that we remember the suffering that Christ endured for us and that He resurrected from the dead and will return. This is the unifying distinction of the Christian religion all over the world.

I had the honor of serving as an assistant to the priest when I was the parish council president in my early 30s. During mass, I helped the priest serve communion as people walked up since there was no longer an altar rail to kneel by.

There was one occasion when a woman with a disability (perhaps muscular dystrophy) came up to receive communion. She somehow lost her balance and grabbed the chalice I was holding, and several communion hosts fell to the floor. I felt terrible as the service came to an abrupt stop. It happened quickly, but in my mind, this shock happened in slow motion. I quickly picked up the hosts, and the priest laid a covering in the area where the wafers had fallen. After the service, the priest examined the floor with his face about an inch above the flooring. He told me he wanted to make sure there was no particles left on the floor. I agonized over this for the following week as I felt like somehow, I had not done my job properly. When I told the priest I did not want to serve communion any longer, we talked, and he was able to convince me to continue helping him.

It was a common practice for young children (at an age before their First Communion) to approach the altar with their parents. It is not proper for young children to receive communion until they fully understand the sanctity of the Lord's Supper. I have a fond memory of blessing young children who approached the altar during communion. I blessed each child by tracing a small cross on their forehead and telling them, "May you always know that Jesus loves you!"

The kids left smiling, and some hugged me before going back to their seats.

Here's a prayer you might say when taking the Lord's Supper:

As I take the bread representing Your life that was broken for me, it is impossible to fathom the pain and suffering of Your crucifixion. Yet, You willingly took that pain for me. You died for me! I am privileged to receive this bread in remembrance of You.

And in the same way, as I take this cup representing Your blood poured out on that rugged cross, I realize that You were the supreme sacrifice for all my sin: past, present, and future. Because of Your blood shed for me, and Your body broken for me, I am free from the power and penalty of sin.

Lord, help me to continue to connect my life, my heart, my thoughts, my everything to You. Fill me today with Your powerful Spirit. As I leave this place, help me to hold this fresh remembrance and the story that never grows old close to my heart. Lead me to share its message of your Last Supper faithfully. In Your Precious name, Amen.

## Baptism

After you have accepted Christ as Lord and Savior, it is important to be immersed in water or baptized. Before Jesus, John the Baptist performed water baptism as a proclamation that the people had been cleansed of our sins by repenting as they were getting ready for the Messiah to appear.

Baptism is a symbolic proclamation that we are joined with Christ in His death and resurrection. Romans 6:3–4 says, *"Or have you forgotten that all of us who were baptized into Christ Jesus were baptized into his death? For we died and were buried with Christ by baptism. And just as Christ was raised from the dead by the glorious power of the Father, now we also may live new lives."*

In other words, we emerged from baptismal water to illustrate Jesus's resurrection from the dead. The old self is gone, and we are a new creation. We have had a change inside of us spiritually — we have been crucified with Jesus, and we no longer live, because it is Christ who lives in us.

Before being baptized at age 47, I was full of excitement and talked to many of the church members. We talked about how important it is for the person being baptized to fully understand the significance of baptism. When children are baptized as infants, they have no recollection when water is poured over their forehead at the baptismal font. I remember Mary Jane teasing me by saying I would be held under water a little longer because of my upbringing.

There was another church member who was somewhat legalistic, and she did not know how to respond when I offered her this suggestion. I told her she could write down her sins on a piece of paper, and I would put the paper in my pocket so they could be immersed in water during my baptism. She did not respond and turned to her husband in disbelief. He knew I was antagonizing her, and he just chuckled enough to keep us both out of trouble.

Just before going into the baptismal font, I told brother Joe that I wanted to keep my eyeglasses on because I wanted to see clearly when I came out of the water. My eyes have been focused and can spiritually see better since that wonderful day.

Baptism is mentioned in Acts 2:38, when Peter said to those present on the Day of Pentecost: *"Repent and let every one of you, be baptized in the name of Jesus Christ for the remission of sins and you shall receive the gift of the Holy Spirit."* It should be noted that Peter is not speaking here of receiving the gift of being able to talk in other languages. Those being baptized receive forgiveness and the indwelling of the Holy Spirit, which is essential for producing the Fruit of the Spirit (Gal. 5:22).

In summary, Baptism is:

- An act of *faith* and *obedience* to the commands of Christ.

*"Therefore, go and make disciples of all nations, baptizing them in the name of the Father and of the Son and of the Holy Spirit, and teaching them to obey everything I have commanded you. And surely, I am with you always, to the very end of the age"* (Matt. 28:19–20).

- A *public declaration* as it proclaims to the world that you are a follower of Jesus Christ.

It is a public confession of your faith in and commitment to Jesus Christ. It is the next step after salvation through repentance and faith and is an important foundation for Christian life.

*Then he said, "Go into the world. Go everywhere and announce the message of God's good news to one and all. Whoever believes and is baptized is saved; whoever refuses to believe is damned"* (Mk. 16:16).

- A move from death to life:

Baptism is a symbol of Christ's burial and resurrection. Our entrance into the water during baptism identifies us with Christ's death on the cross, His burial in the tomb, and His resurrection from the dead.

Most importantly, water baptism is a symbol of your new life as a Christian. We bury the "old life," and we rise to walk in a "new life." Thank you, Jesus!

## Be a Witness

As followers of Christ, we have been commanded to tell others about Him. Just before the Lord ascended into Heaven, he gave final instructions to the eleven remaining apostles. *"He said to them, 'Go into all the world and preach the good news to all creation'"* (Mk. 16:15). After He had spoken to them, he was taken up into Heaven, where He sits at the right hand of the Father.

"America's Pastor" Billy Graham preached the gospel in person to almost 215 million people in 185 countries between 1937 and 2013.[11] He reached hundreds of millions more through radio, television, newspaper columns, magazines, books, films, and webcasts. His life (1918–2018) demonstrated his commitment to preaching the good news throughout the world. His quote that follows tells of his passion for sharing God's love: "I am convinced the greatest act of love we can ever perform for people is to tell them about God's love for them in Christ."

There have been times when I've talked to others about Jesus, and we have had different opinions. I've learned to stay in the spirit of Love and tell others about what believing in Christ has done in my life. I've learned to recognize when people don't want to hear about it and save the good news for another day. Sometimes I may tell them a story just to give them something to chew on until the next time we talk. It is a travesty when people just blindly follow beliefs that have no biblical foundation. It is also an injustice when those who preach the Word do it solely for monetary gain. It is critical for all of us to stay grounded in the Word of God. When you are not sure on what the answer is, open your Bible, do your research—the Truth is there! The more you read it, the better you become equipped to share His Love with others.

## Flying High for Jesus

One of my opportunities to witness happened on a plane headed for Harlingen, Texas, around 2001. That year, I had earned a companion pass for Irma because of my frequent flights. She was able to accompany me on flights at no cost. On this occasion, we were flying into southern Texas. I was intrigued at the time by a book called *The Prayer of Jabez*. That day I had prayed to meet a person on the plane who needed to hear about Jesus. It became a more specific and bold prayer when I asked for that person to be seated next to me. When Irma and I looked for our seats, we settled in a row with only two seats. I thought to myself, "I guess I will not be meeting a person that needs to hear about Jesus" as I looked at Irma sitting next to me. The flight was full and just before the doors were closed for takeoff, a young couple rushed into the plane and appeared to be arguing. They ended up being seated near the back of the plane on separate rows. Once they crammed their carry-on luggage into the slivers of remaining space in the overhead compartments, we were ready for takeoff.

The flight was without incident, but things changed quickly when we began our descent. I saw a flight attendant go into the cockpit and then hurry out. She proceeded to the middle of the plane and looked through an opening (peek hole) on the floor that I had never previously noticed was there. She was examining the wheels on the plane that are lowered when the plane lands. She scampered back into the cockpit and just moments afterward, the pilot made the following announcement: "Hello, this is the captain. We are having a mechanical problem with the plane. Our wheels do not appear to be locked into the proper position for landing. The flight attendants will be giving instructions on how to prepare for emergency landing!" My mind immediately raced to Psalm 23 and began trying to calm Irma and myself as we prayed for whatever was going to happen next. Irma pulled out whatever paper she had in her purse and began writing farewell messages to her sons, Steve and Anthony. The moment was surreal, and it seemed like all the passengers on the plane were holding their breath at the same time. The flight attendant stood in the middle of the aisle and nervously said, "I need three men to assist me in the back of the plane!" When I looked around, no one was moving, some men pretended to be asleep while other men latched onto their spouses like hungry ticks. I told Irma, "I need to help them!" She reluctantly said, "I know." After we blessed each other, I headed toward the back of the plane. I tried to encourage her by saying, "I'll see you in a little while." It felt like the walk to the rear of the plane took forever.

The stewardess huddled us three volunteers and gave us our individual assignments. The first volunteer was to help the flight attendant open the emergency back door and throw it away from the plane. The second man was told to help others and try to keep them calm. My assignment was to block the aisle in case there was a stampede. I remember, the flight attendant's eyes filling with tears of self-pity and saying, "If something should happen to me, just push me to the side." I bluntly responded, "We can do that!" and we took our positions. I sat near the window; the man sitting next to me was the young man who entered the plane last and had been arguing with his wife. On the aisle seat was the man who had the assignment of opening the emergency back door. There was an air of nervous energy that sent shock waves throughout the airplane.

The captain announced the airport was aware of our situation and emergency responders were already in place on the runway. As we waited for our fate, the man next to me asked me if I was scared, and I responded, "No!" Then it hit me like a splash of holy water on my face, this man sitting next to me is the one that needs to hear about Jesus. My fear vanished like a genie retreating into his magic lamp. I felt alert and alive and asked the man next to me, "If you were to die today, would you go to Heaven?" He angrily responded, "Are you messin' with me, man?" It was somewhat awkward because we were seated so close together. I responded that I was serious and asked him again to answer my question. He nervously said, "I'll be okay, I've studied Eastern philosophy." I chuckled and said, "That's not going to get it, you need to hear about Jesus!" I went into my quick and concise version in leading someone to salvation, a version that I had never practiced or used before.

My two-minute drill took biblical steps, something I had learned previously referred to as the Roman Route. You can follow this path and use it as a guide to tell someone about Christ. These are the verses: Romans 3:23, Romans 6:23, John 3:3, John 14:6, and ends with Romans 10:9–10. Note to reader: Please look them up and take time to meditate on each of these verses. A woman sitting in the row in front of me extended her hand toward us and winked as she became my silent prayer partner during this encounter. By the time I finished reading Romans 10:10, *"For it is with your heart that you believe and are justified, and it is with your mouth that you confess and are saved,"* the man responded as if he were begging not

119

have his head cut off. "Yes! Yes! I believe in Jesus!" He then regained composure and asked me, "What's going to happen next?" I told him the plane would attempt a landing, and if the wheels did not engage properly, we would skid down the runway on the belly of the plane until it stops. I reassured him there was emergency personnel waiting for us.

At this point, we were given instructions to go into the brace position for emergency landing. I knew we were going to be okay, and I confidently looked around the plane. I could no longer see anyone over the seats in front of me as everyone had leaned forward and locked their arms under their legs.

I looked out the window and felt the plane touch the runway like all previous landings I had ever previously experienced. I felt like ru**Ben-Hur** taking his victory lap around the Colosseum in Rome. The man seated next to me started screaming, "We're sliding! We're sliding!" I told him to be quiet as he was going to scare the other passengers. The passengers gave a round of applause when the captain announced, "The eagle has landed!" I was filled with a chest full of joy and gratitude that my Jabez prayer was answered and I got to tell someone about Jesus.

The young man next to me looked in disbelief and exclaimed, "I cannot believe you were not afraid!" I responded, "That's because I know where I am going when I die; I know when I become absent in my body, I will be present with the Lord. You need to get ready, you believed for a moment only out of desperation!"

He then responded, "Who are you, a minister or something?"

I proudly announced, "No, I am the postmaster of McAllen, Texas!" It was hilarious even though I did not mean it to be.

I gave him my business card and wrote down several scriptures. I gave him further advice by saying it would benefit him to look up these verses when he got home. I asked him to keep in touch but never heard from him again.

As I met up with Irma, we were on opposite ends on the spectrum of emotions. I was bubbling and full of excitement as I told her what happened in the back of the plane. She was tearful and began telling me about the emotional messages she had written to her sons. The airline personnel inside the airport showed an abundance of empathy as we exited the airplane. We were given forms by the airline to fill out to release them of any injury that may have occurred during this flight. My businessman shrewdness took over as I requested two flights anywhere as compensation for this ordeal. We received the vouchers for two flights in the continental US within a few days. Telling others about Jesus is exciting and sometimes *sharper than any double-edged sword, it penetrates even to dividing soul and spirit, joints and marrow.* We must be ready to tell anyone the Good News during any occasion and every season of our life. My prayer today is that I keep my eyes wide open, so I do not miss any opportunity to share how He pulled me out of the darkness. Even though I did not deserve it, He forgave me of my sins and loved this dead man back to life. He turned my heart of stone into one that is full of His Love. He can do the same for you; do not be someone who turns away from the living God. Tell someone to make a decision *today*! *"As long as it called TODAY, so that none of you will be hardened by sin's deceitfulness"* (Heb. 3:13).

**Golden Step #9: Partake in the Lord's Supper regularly, get baptized, and tell others the Good News.**

# CHAPTER 10

## BEAR MUCH FRUIT

*"I am the vine; you are the branches. If you remain in Me and I in you, you will <u>bear much fruit</u>; apart from Me you can do nothing"* (Jn. 15:5).

P art of getting set to go to Heaven is to discover your go-to, or favorite, scripture. The above scripture is the one I have chosen as my compass and stabilizer in this journey called life. It helps me stay focused on what is most important to me, and that is to first remain in Jesus. The outcome of abiding in Him will have evidence of fruit. At this point, I want you to think about which scripture is your covering for your daily walk. It is also important to ask yourself what in your life is most important to you. When you figure this out, have the courage to build your life around that answer. My answer is to abide in Jesus and He in Me because without him I can do nothing and will have no fruit to share. John 15:5 also keeps a song in my heart and a smile on my face so I can beam His Goodness.

Here's a little trivia about me from back in the 1950s. Did you know that my nickname as a young boy was Ruben Bear? My closest cousins including my bestest (Dianna) know this. My cousin Danny Bear and I would wrestle like cubs when we could "bearly" walk. We were so happy to see each other that we hugged, and then we tumbled over into a wrestling contest. I am so glad to know that Danny and I are on the same Golden Walk and will one day wrestle in Heaven (I hope he is still skinny so I can pin him). As far as my bestest, she used to only share her honey with my sister Lupe and myself. I am confident the three of us will share the sweetness of Heaven together when God calls us Home. My cousins were the children of Joe and Tillie Gonzales. Joe was my father's first cousin, and Tillie was my mom's sister. Our parents are waiting for us in Heaven along with my cousin Joe, who is part of the chain to link us all there. So, from oldest to youngest, these are my cousins' names: Joe, Bobby, David, Pete, Danny, Dianna, Alfie, Michael, Paul, and Lizzie. My *tíos* also had a baby boy named Mark, who died at the age of 18 months. God bless you, my cousins/*primos hermanos*! My frosties! See you up there!

What does it mean to bear fruit? The answer is found in Galatians 5:22: *"But the fruit of the spirit is love, joy, peace, patience, kindness, goodness, gentleness, faithfulness and self-control."*

During nine consecutive days of postings on Facebook about the Fruit of the Spirit, I wrote nine parts to a poem for each of the fruits. Below you will find the complete poem (written between August 4 and 12, 2019) named "Fruit of the Spirit":

Only one life and it goes by so fast
Fill it with **LOVE** to make memories that last
Making **PEACE** with ourselves is always a must
Forgiving our enemies gains us God's trust
Receive **JOY** and peace that you can't fully understand
By accepting Jesus and following His command

Lord, give me **PATIENCE**, like only You know how
I need it really bad; I can't wait ... I need it right now
Spread some **KINDNESS** by smiling at someone who is down
You might be surprised to witness a vanishing frown
Domestic violence and hatred has our country in an uproar
Counter with **GOODNESS** and prayers till we reach the Narrow Door
Treat others with **GENTLENESS** like the Holy Dove
Sharing the Blessings that come from Our Father above
Our **FAITHFULNESS** will be rewarded when the race is finally won
Like candy for our ears when we hear Him say, "Enter, well done!"
The world is watching, we must fulfill our role
Show some Wisdom United: practice **SELF-CONTROL**
Eternal Fruit of the Spirit for toddler to grandpa
Because against such things there is no law

At this time I must point out the fruit of the spirit is in complete contrast to the acts of the flesh. *"The acts of the flesh are obvious: sexual immorality, impurity and debauchery, idolatry and witchcraft; hatred, discord, jealousy, fits of rage, selfish ambition, dissensions, factions and envy; drunkenness, orgies and the like. I warn you, as I did before, that those who live like this will not inherit the Kingdom of God"* (Gal. 5:19–22). God in His mercy pulled me out of a filthy grave. The Son has set me free, so the forecast calls for only good days ahead.

Here are several basic steps to avoid sin while getting set to go to Heaven:

- Get into the Bible: it contains **B**asic **I**nstructions **B**efore **L**eaving **E**arth.

- Trust God and have faith in His promises

- Be aware of what causes you to sin, and then pray. Learn and hide the Word in your heart so you will not sin.

- Take responsibility for your actions—you know what is right and what is wrong.

- Turn your back on sins from the past. Strive to never make the same mistakes again.

- Ask God for forgiveness and forgive others, including yourself.

- Be more like Jesus and less like your old self.

- Glorify God with your actions and stay on the path of His purpose for you.

- Rejoice because immortality in Heaven is our reward.

There is a hidden gem found in Psalm 107 that has to do with sailors trapped in a storm. While at sea, *"They reeled and staggered like drunken men; they were at their wits end. Then they cried out to the Lord in their trouble, and He brought them out of their distress. He stilled the storm to a whisper and the waves of the sea to a hush. They were glad when it grew calm, and He guided them to their desired haven"* (Ps. 107:27–30).

Whether the storms in life are of our own making or they come because of living in a broken world, God is greater than any storm. He can calm any storm including the one that may be raging inside of us. All you must do is call out to him because *"Everyone who calls upon the name of the Lord will be saved"* (Rom. 10:13).

I am going to enjoy the Sonshine while God reigns no matter what storms I face. Every day, shine for Jesus, the storm will go away. Shine like the moon as it reflects His Sonlight.

## He Left the Light On!

*"And it was so. God made two great lights …God set them in the vault of the sky to give light on the earth, to govern the day and night, and to* separate *light from darkness. And God saw that it was good"* (Gen. 1:15–16).

Have you ever wondered why the moon shines at night? The answer is easy: it's because God made it that way. Unlike a lamp or our sun, the moon does not produce its own light. Moonlight is actually sunlight that shines on the moon and bounces off. The light reflects off old volcanoes, craters, and lava flows on the moon's surface. The moon does not shine on its own like the sun, nor can we be a reflection without the Son to *separate* light from darkness and illuminate the earth. What are you doing *today* to reflect some "Sonlight" into the dark side of humanity? Our purpose on earth is to separate light from darkness as long as we have breath until the very end.

When I was in the Navy, I used to love to spend time alone on the ship and just lie on the deck and look up at the moon and the stars. I was in awe of the vastness and creation God made for us when He said, *"Let there be light"* in Genesis 1:3. From Broken Walk: "Nighttime on a ship is a fantastic experience. Just being able to see countless stars and thinking about God keeping the whole universe under control. Among all His planets and stars, He chose the Earth and supplied it with air, water, and food, prior to creating us in His image. God keeps the entire expanding universe in His complete control. Our little solar system seems to be doing a perpetual, synchronized dance. The other planets and moons waltz with the Earth in perfect unison around the sun." Close your eyes for a moment and give God thanks for creating us.

The moon's surface is actually dark even though it appears very bright when hanging suspended in the night sky. We, as humans, also are dark until we become a new creation by accepting Jesus as Lord and Savior. Let me explain, from Broken Walk, "It all began when God gave Adam and Eve a soul in the Garden of Eden. *'Then the Lord God formed a man from the dust of the ground and breathed life into his nostrils, the breath of life, and the man became a living being'* (Gen. 2:7)." We, like Adam, all have a soul. Our problem is: we, like Adam, have used our soul to disobey God throughout our lives. As a result of their disobedience, Adam and Eve were kicked out of the Garden of Eden.

As a consequence, we, like Adam and Eve, are not able to get back into the Garden (Heaven) without belief in Jesus. I use scripture, not my words, to shine light on my point: He left the light on. *"Consequently, just as one trespass resulted in condemnation for all people, so also one righteous act resulted in justification and life for all people. For just as through the disobedience of the one man the many were made sinners, so also through the obedience of the One Man the many will be made righteous"* (Rom. 5:18–19). The light shines brightly on this scripture, let it be a river that nourishes the root system of your heart. It is plain to see the one disobedient man is Adam and the obedient man is our Lord and Savior, Jesus Christ.

The offer of life through Jesus remains for us. Make a bright choice *today* and separate yourself from the darkness. He left the light on!

Here are some scripture references to further get a mouthful of the Fruit of the Spirit:

**Love** – His command is that you walk in love: **2 John 6.**
**Joy** – For the Joy of the Lord is your strength:
**Nehemiah 8:10.**
**Peace** – Let the Peace of Christ rule in your hearts:
**Colossians 3:15.**
**Patience** – Be patient with everyone: **1 Thessalonians 5:14.**
**Kindness** – Be kind and compassionate to one another:
**Ephesians 4:32.**
**Goodness** – As we have opportunity, let us do good:
**Galatians 6:10.**
**Gentleness** – Let your gentleness be evident to all:
**Philippians 4:5.**
**Faithfulness** – A faithful man shall abound with blessings:
**Proverbs 28:20.**
**Self-control** – To live self-controlled, upright, and Godly lives: **Titus 2:12.**

There is an old saying that goes, "The apple does not fall far from the tree." If we are abiding in Christ and He in us, we will have evidence of His pods all around us. On the other hand, if we are engaged in the acts of the flesh, we will be into worldly sin and walking in darkness. My prayer is that the Lord plants a seed of kindness in our hearts and it grows so big we can share with everyone.

The phrase "The apple doesn't fall far from the tree" means a child has a similar character and/or qualities to his or her parents. In other words, when you are a child of the

King, you bear the qualities and characteristics of the Fruit of the Spirit. That's exactly where we need to abide and become more like Jesus.

When I was walking in darkness, my heart was full of bad things. I know what love is because I know what love isn't. Without the benefit of having the solid foundation based on His Word, I knew something was wrong but did not know how to fix it. I was in total darkness and had not been to a church in 8 years. Here's part of my story when I first called out to God. This excerpt is taken from *Broken Walk*:

St Patrick's Cathedral is the largest decorated neo-gothic Catholic cathedral in North America. It can accommodate 3,000 people and was built in 1879 of brick clad in marble. It is a spectacular building as it takes up a whole city block. It is located directly across from Rockefeller Center and considered one of the most visible symbols of Roman Catholicism in New York City and the United States. It has a total of 19 bells weighing more than 29,000 pounds. So this seemed like an excellent choice in which to go back to church after an eight-year hiatus. Besides, it was only a 5-minute walk from the Waldorf-Astoria.

Once inside the church, my mood became solemn as I could smell a mixture of burning candles and incense. A flash of being an altar boy at Our Lady of Fatima in Phoenix sped through my mind. It was incredible to see the stained-glass windows and ornate decorations inside this magnificent edifice. It did not take long for my spiritual attention to connect to the great I Am as I silently prayed in the state of humility and remorse. Somehow, even though the cathedral was filling, I was all alone with God. "But when you pray, go into your room, close the door and pray to your Father who is unseen. Then your Father, who sees what is done in secret, will reward you" (Matt. 6:6).

Before too long, my tears started to flow as I examined my current state of who I presently was. I did not like myself and wanted to change, but I needed help. In the pit of my stomach, I knew my relationship with my family, especially my sons, was ruined, and I did not know how to fix it. It made me realize there was a hole in my heart that had been plastered with financial and occupational success. Somehow these distractions did little to stop the bleeding and agony within my core. The band-aid for my emotions over the past eight years had been to work long hours during the work week and then fill the weekends with drinking and gambling. I was addicted to all three of these activities. During my time of reflection, there was a Mass taking place around me, but I was unaware as I was bent over in a pile of tearful sentiments. My throat burned from bile that had made its way to my tonsils. As I cried, it felt like my heart was about to come out of my chest. It felt like the arteries wanted to come outside of my body and somehow grab and cling like vines to God. I begged God for a solution, but it was a one-way conversation. I silently, but wholeheartedly, called out for God to change my situation. At that time, I was not familiar with the promise in Romans 10:13 that says, "Everyone who calls upon the name of the Lord will be saved." The word "saved" is not only about salvation (getting to go to Heaven). It also means being restored to wholeness while you are being healed spiritually and physically. When you sincerely confess with your mouth and believe in your heart that Jesus is Lord and God raised Him from the dead, you begin a personal relationship with Christ.

When I realized there were people around me, I was hoping someone would talk to me. One by one, they left, and no one offered encouragement or a pat on the back. After the mass was over and the church had emptied, I saw the priest looking at me from the pulpit. I was hoping he would offer a gesture of consolation, but he stayed away from me as if I had the COVID-19 virus. I felt completely spent as I hobbled out of the church with my head down and my eyes swollen. It seemed like I was the only person on earth and there was no one around to help me. *Not even God*!

After I returned to Little Rock, Arkansas, God worked quickly and took me away from the darkness and soon afterward immersed me in His Marvelous Light.

## <u>Bearing Fruit</u>

That's enough about me, let's talk about what you can do while you are getting ready to go to Heaven. My wife and I use the expression "Food equals **love**." If you see someone who is hungry, give him or her food to eat. A "Point-in-Time-Count" taken in America in 2019 estimated there are 557,715 people experiencing homelessness on a given night.[12] You can look up these numbers on HUD's Annual Point-in-Time Count.

Let the *peace* of Christ rule in your heart because *"a heart at peace gives life to the body"* (Prov. 25:14). Be ready to listen with compassion when someone is voicing their current distress. Many times, a troubled person just needs to be heard rather than presented with an answer. Peace begins with you when you welcome peace into yourself by inviting the Prince of *Peace* to live in your heart.

*"The Joy of the Lord is our strength"* (Neh. 8:10). Reflect His *joy* using the strength He has given you. When you see someone that needs a hand, be an extension of His Hands. Think of *JOY* meaning Jesus, Others, Yourself, in that order. Remember, God loves to hear us sing even if we are off-key. He listens to the sincerity of the song from your heart. And

He loves to hear the music that harmonizes with the way you live your life.

We must trust in God's perfect timing even when we want something right now. My prayer is for more *patience* to allow His fullness and glory to be evident in our lives. We must learn to be still and let the Potter refine us into His finished product, not ours. We might be waiting for a new direction in our career, for a relationship to be restored, or for the willpower to break a bad habit. Put your trust in God — He hears, and He will deliver in His time.

We live in a world when sometimes hate becomes loud; we must counter it by making *kindness* louder than hate. Demonstrate God's love to someone who is hurting or discouraged. Be *kind* to the unkind! Isn't that what God did for us? Offer a word of encouragement, write a note that gives someone affirmation. We can't change the world, but we can influence those around us. It begins by recognizing sometimes the one we need to change is looking back at us in the mirror.

Good deeds should be given as a form a worship out of the abundance of our heart in gratefulness to reflect the *goodness* of God in our lives. We are blessed to be a blessing! God knows when we give with good intentions. Our generosity must be motivated by love as we give Him all the glory, honor, and praise. Highlighting our giving with the expectation of being honored will take the focus off the Giver of all things — Jesus.

We must learn to think before we react. We can follow the example of Jesus when the Pharisees brought Him a woman caught committing adultery. The Pharisees wanted her stoned to death, and some already had a rock in their hand. Jesus responded with *gentleness* by saying, *"Let him without sin cast the first stone"* (Jn. 8:7). The next sound heard (besides crickets) was the *gentleness* of rocks hitting the ground, one by one, dropped by the Pharisees before they left the scene.

God loves us so much He sent His Son to make a way for us to be able to enter Heaven. The least we can do in gratitude is to share our *faithfulness* with others. Thank you, Lord, for pouring out Your love for us through your death on the cross. Help us show our *faithfulness* by sharing your gift of salvation to those we meet in life.

Learn how to recognize what is going to make you sin and then, avoid it. I know I make it sound easy, but being aware of it is your first line of defense in *self-control*. Remember who reigns in your heart—Jesus. Greater is the One living inside of me than the one who is in the world. Thank you, Lord, for being greater than any temptation that comes at us. Please teach us to recognize it and provide us with a way out. Ask yourself if the underlying factor you have is because you don't want to lose control. Maybe you have a fear of flying because of the loss of control. Here's a way to fix being a control freak: next time you are on a plane, knock on the cockpit door and tell the pilot you want to fly the plane. LOL.

The fruit of the spirit are the qualities that are evident when living an abundant life in Christ. Think of it as a beautiful painting for all to see for His Glory. It can be thought of as your favorite and most flavorful fruit perfectly painted on a canvass made of love. The fruit of the spirit comes directly from God with pure, faultless quality; it is bursting with His Love for us. *"Against such thing there is no Law!"* (Gal. 5:23).

As a body of Christ waiting to go to Heaven, we must be bold about our faith. We must have fire in our bones and follow the example of the prophet Elijah that had so much fire in him that he challenged the priests of the phony god Baal to a showdown. It is an incredible story found in 1 Kings 18:20–40. When Elijah prayed, fire came down from Heaven, and he was victorious. He stood up for God that day, and we cannot be afraid to speak up for God today. We must be a spark that creates fire to come down from Heaven.

**Golden Step #10: Abide in Him and bear much fruit.**

# CHAPTER 11

## BY FAITH

*"By faith we understand that the universe was formed at God's command, so that what is seen was not made out of what is visible"* (Heb. 11:2).

Look around at everything you see including your family members; before God's command, there was nothing. Our faith begins with the very first verse in the Bible — In the beginning God created the heavens and earth. The second verse describes how the earth was formless and empty with darkness. It was just the beginning as the Spirit of God was hovering over the waters. Then God commanded, "Let there be light," and the light penetrated the darkness. In the beginning was the Word (Jesus) and through Him all things were made. In Him (Jesus) was life, and that life is the light of all mankind. This light outshines all darkness, and the darkness will never overcome the light. *Do you believe that?* I do, it is the foundation of my faith. He is the Alpha and the Omega, always was and always will be. To those who believe in Him, He gave the right to become children of God. He made it possible, *by faith*, for us to live in Heaven forever. Heaven is forever, but unfortunately, so is hell.

We are now in Chapter 11 of this book; if you still have not accepted Christ as your Lord and Savior, it is time to file a form of spiritual Chapter 11. In the physical realm, individuals and businesses can file Chapter 11 (bankruptcy) when their debts overcome their ability to pay. It is a legal process through the court system where the person/business in debt files a petition for debt relief.

How about in spiritual bankruptcy? At some point in our life, we need to pull out our white flag and put our trust in God. He did His part by sending his Son to live and dwell among us as flesh and then die on the cross. By His blood, the stain of our sins were washed away. By faith, we must acknowledge we can't pay for our debt (sin). We cannot get to Heaven without sending up a white flag from our heart and then asking Jesus to save us. How do we do this? Romans 10 tells us how: *"'The word is near you; it is in your mouth and in your heart,' that is the message concerning _faith_ that we proclaim: If you declare with your mouth, 'Jesus is Lord,' and believe in your heart that God raised Him from the dead, you will be saved"* (Rom. 10:8–10). Keep in mind, Jesus is the same Lord for *all* and richly blesses *all* who call on Him. Jesus is the Way, the Truth, and the Life—no one gets to Heaven except through Him. Raise that white flag from the depths of your soul and surrender to His Lordship now and forevermore.

According to the Bible in Hebrews 11:1, *"Faith is having confidence in what we hope for and assurance in what we do not see."* We can say we trust God completely with our heart, mind, and soul, but those are words. Faith is demonstrated when you trust God during impossible times with your action. Sometimes God tests our trust to see how good we are at trusting him. Whatever the situation in your life, it is faith in God the Almighty that helps you overcome. It gives you power over your condition as you give control to Him.

*Faith can bring you out of any hardship or condition* you may be facing.

Unbelief is what makes you stay in the wilderness, just like the Israelites did for forty years. (Look up this story in Numbers Chapters 13 and 14. There is also more on this in Deuteronomy 1 and 2.) Digging into your Bible is all part of getting set to go to Heaven.

There are three main parts to live *by faith:*

- **Believing Christ**: Establish trust in Him by agreeing that God sent Him to us. He sacrificed His life for us and then rose from the dead. Surrendering to His Lordship and giving Him full control is called believing in Him.

- **Knowing Christ**: Learn all you can about Jesus, through the scriptures. Study His miracles and promises. Find wisdom in His parables and lessons. Study the way He glorified the Father.

- **Living like Him**: After establishing your belief in Him, forget your past life and go forward in life as a new creation. You no longer live as yourself as it is Christ living in you. You live for Him and prove it by your actions that resemble Him. You stand firm and never give up even in the worst of times. Always shine His light to glorify God.

There are so many examples of faith throughout the Bible, especially in Hebrews, Chapter 11.

My favorite story of faith is about *the boy who stood against the Giant*, found in 1 Samuel Chapter 17.

The people of Philistine always wanted to conquer Israel and defeat their army, so they gathered their soldiers together for battle. King Saul and the armies of Israel also assembled their troops together to prepare for battle. The Philistines stood on a mountain side on one side, and Israel stood on a mountain on the other side.

In the valley of Elah, there were separate camps with tents that housed both Israelites and Philistines. For forty days, morning and evening, a giant named Goliath (a champion) came out of the tent shouting at the Israelites to face him. Goliath called for a battle where the outcome was to have two opposing champions fight to the death. This was a winner-take-all contest—as it was believed to be the will of the gods by the Philistines. "Goliath stood and shouted to the ranks of Israel, *'Why do you come out and line up for battle? Am I not a Philistine, and are you not servants of Saul? Choose a man and have him come down to me. If he is able to fight and kill me, we will become your subjects; but if I overcome him and kill him, you will become our subjects and serve us'"* (1 Sam. 17:8–9). Saul, the king of Israel, was there with his army, but everyone, including the king, feared the giant. They did not step forward to fight Goliath. The giant was nine feet and nine inches tall and *"had a bronze helmet on his head, and he was armed with a coat of scale amour, and the weight of the coat was five thousand shekels of bronze"* (1 Sam. 17:5; 5000 shekels weigh 125 pounds, probably close to the weight of the boy named David).

David was a shepherd who came to visit his brothers who were soldiers in the Israeli army. He heard the giant's taunts and decided to fight Goliath and defeat him. David was deeply annoyed by the giant and the fear displayed by the Israeli soldiers. David questioned, *"Who is this uncircumcised Philistine, that he should defy the armies of the living God?"*

(1 Sam. 17:26). David's oldest brother Eliab was angry and jealous about David going against the giant. David was taken to the king, who offered him a sword, armor, and shield to protect himself. But David said he would fight in his own way. David could not walk in Saul's anointing or battle gear. Besides, the battle was the Lord's, and He does not save with sword and spear.

David prayed to God and then went forward to call the giant after *"he chose for himself five smooth stones from the brook and put them in his shepherd's bag, in a pouch which he had, and his sling was in his hand"* (1 Sam. 17:40). History has proven that the most powerful weapon is the spoken Word of God. David yelled at Goliath, *"You come against me with sword and spear and javelin, but I come against you in the name of the Lord Almighty...This day the Lord will hand you over to me, and I'll strike you down and cut off your head. Today I will give the carcasses of the Philistine army to the birds of the air and the beasts of the earth, and the whole world will know there is a God in Israel"* (1 Sam. 17:45–46). God gave him a plan, and David struck the giant's head from far away with a stone. The giant fell and became weak as his face hit the ground. David quickly ran toward Goliath and killed him with the giant's own sword and cut off his head off with it. All the Philistines saw the fight and ran away in terror. David became the hero of Israel only because of his faith in God. He was unarmed but still able to knock down the giant because he trusted God would help him. David's defeat of the giant demonstrates to us that having firm faith helps us to battle any big obstacle we are facing. There is no adversity in life that can stand against the Word of God. A scripture verse hidden in your heart can be the stone to knock down any giant we face.

No matter what you are facing, if we pray and have faith, God can help us defeat the giants that come in the form of divorce, debt, job loss, death of a loved one, illness, anxiety, addiction, pornography, incest, pedophilia, poverty, loneliness, incarceration, betrayal, wanting revenge, unforgiveness, and unbelief. *Trust God and let Him fight your battles.*

## Facing the Robber with a Rock

Way back in the dinosaur days in the summer of 1968, I had decided to no longer attend the seminary after two years of study. Here's an excerpt from *Broken Walk:*

When I looked behind me, none of my co-workers were there as they had tired-out chasing the man who had just robbed the store. I do not remember when I picked up a large rock during this chase to defend myself. I was surprised when the robber turned and growled at me in an alley close to Buck's market, *"Boy, whatcha gonna do with that rock!"* I was about 10 feet from him and felt sheer terror saturating my 16-year-old body. I was frozen like a statue and I could not talk. Then, by the grace of God, my unexpected guardian angel showed up. A man stepped out of a gate from his back yard and had a rifle pointed at the robber. He screamed, "Don't you do anything to that boy!" My God-commanded protector held him at gunpoint until the police arrived.

This was one of the first angels I remember protecting me during my life. It happened about two weeks after I started my first job at Moe's Food Fair Market. This was my first official job other than being a paper punk (newspaper delivery boy). I was a naive 16-year-old, fresh out of the seminary, trying to adjust to my new environment back in the hood. The store manager had just yelled out into the public announcement system, "The store has been robbed, we need to catch the robber." We did not include him, and the chase was on. Since I had been playing soccer regularly, I quickly caught up with the winded store robber all by myself. Reality hit as the adrenaline from the chase instantly turned into fear as I tried to figure out what to do next. It was music to my ears when I heard the angel's Pavarotti voice yell, "Don't you do anything to that boy!" The robber backed away from me and stood there without moving until the police arrived. There have been several angel incidents during my life, some of which I did not see.

Back then, even though I had attended a seminary for two years, my faith and trust in God was not fully developed. God had a plan for my life, and He has helped in many situations that seemed impossible throughout my life. For this, I am forever grateful.

The Bible teaches that our faith pleases God more than anything else. Here is a list of characters of faith that every Christian can learn about to build their faith and increase their trust in God. These are must-reads. It is *up to you* as part of getting set to go to Heaven to look up and read these wonderful examples of faith.

1. Abraham: *"believed God, and it was accounted to him for righteousness." Therefore, know that <u>only</u> those who are of <u>faith</u> are sons of Abraham"* Galatians 3:6–7. Also read Genesis Chapter 22 for an ultimate example of *faith*.

2. Shadrach, Meshach, and Abednego: Their faith is tested in a fiery furnace in Daniel Chapter 3.

3. Esther: The brave Jewish queen demonstrates her faith over fear in the Book of Esther.

4. Noah proves his faith by building an ark to save his household. He was 600 years old in the year the flood

came. He built the ark not knowing what rain was, as it had never rained on earth yet. Genesis Chapters 6–10.

5. Jonah cries out in faith from the belly of a fish. Book of Jonah

6. Joseph is a beautiful story of a life full of faith. Genesis Chapters 37–48

7. David killed Goliath as a young shepherd boy by faith. 1 Samuel Chapter 17

8. The woman with an issue of blood shows how she responds with action by faith. Matthew 9:20.

9. Daniel survived the lion's den by having faith in God. Daniel Chapter 6.

10. Moses became Israel's greatest prophet by faith. Deuteronomy 34:10–12.

11. Nicodemus became a believer of Christ through faith. John Chapter 3 and John 19:39.

12. Paul went from Christian killer to Christ follower by faith. Acts Chapter 9.

13. Rahab, the prostitute, was able to spare her family through her shield of faith. Joshua 6:22–25.

14. Job was restored in double portions because of his impeccable faith. Book of Job.

15. Gideon subdues the Midianites with 300 men by faith.
    Judges Chapter 8.

There are many more fascinating Bible characters. I'm
providing the above list so you can look up these 15 heroes
and get encouraged when you see how God can use anyone
for His Kingdom. Be like a miner digging for gold when
you explore the mines filled with precious ore. Dig into this
remarkable love letter from God, and you will find hidden
treasures. Store these nuggets of wisdom and pearls of faith
in the vault of your heart. Unlike other books, the words
in the Bible are made alive through the power of the Holy
Spirit. These inspirational Bible stories about faith help us
stay strong during our hard times.

*Have you had your Gideon moment*? A Gideon moment
comes when you ask God to show you a sign so you can
believe. Gideon asked God to wet the fleece with dew but
not wet the ground. The next day, he then requests of God to
wet the ground with dew but not the fleece...God does both.
My Gideon moment came early on as a brand-new believer.

My head was spinning since I was learning so much as I
was immersed in the living water of the Word. I wondered
whether I would be able to stop drinking. Will I be able to
stop swearing? What will my colleagues think of me? Will
my family accept my decision? How can I afford to tithe
when I don't have enough now? What about gambling?
What do I do next? This is when I received the instruction to
buy my first Bible and read from it *every day*.

During my Sunday school lessons for new believers, I
was taught that it was imperative for me to read the Bible
every day, so I bought my first Bible. After struggling with
reading the Bible every day and not knowing on how to
begin, I sighed and gave a mental eye roll. I had my Gideon

moment, and I prayed something like this, "Dear God, if you are real and your word is true, show me some proof." I continued this prayer by saying, "When I open my new Bible for the first time and touch whatever verse I land on, show me something that will increase my faith." What happened next has led me to read my bible *every* day for the past nineteen-plus years.

When I carefully opened my bible, my finger landed on Hebrews 4:12. It says, "*The word of God is alive and active. Sharper than any double-edged sword, it penetrates even to dividing soul and spirit, joints and marrow, it judges the thoughts and attitudes of the heart.*" I was stunned and cried for nearly an hour as I knew this was not a coincidence but God caring enough for me to take me to this *powerful verse*. This was the first time in my life I felt oily tears flowing from my eyes. These tears seemed to cleanse my soul of all skepticism and disbelief. Hmm, here's a thought: If the eyes are a window to our soul, then perhaps our tears serve as the extra ingredient to see into Heaven.

Reading in the good book made me reexamine my beliefs.

What is it that you truly believe? In *getting set* to go to Heaven only you can prevent eternal fires! Sounds like a Smokey the Bear quote. LOL. Seriously, take time to *do your research* on what you have been taught. Is it in the Bible or is it something that someone said is in the Bible? *Is it a promise* from God or *is it a manipulation* from a false teacher? For example, I was taught in 1966 that if I completed a nine-month novena/prayer to the patron saint on a colorful bookmark on the first Friday of consecutive months, my admission to Heaven was guaranteed. What do you think? I'll give you my truck and my Keurig if you can find this *mendacious teaching* in the scriptures.

Test what you have been taught by looking it up in the Bible. How about, *"If you write a check out in the amount of $54.17, no weapon formed against you will prosper!"* Is it in the Bible? Part of the words are there in Isaiah 54:17, but it does not come with having to write a check to a false teacher for fifty-four dollars and seventeen cents. Dig into the word, the truth will set you free. *"I am as happy over Your promise as if I had found a great treasure"* (Ps. 119:162). Lord, thank you for the treasure of the Bible. Please touch our hearts with an unquenchable desire to dive deep into your Word *every day*.

Knowing God is our greatest treasure; learning about Him in scripture is easier than finding gold. Just begin by praying, and then open your heart and open your Bible. God is there waiting for you, just waiting to be found. His name is just one letter away from gold and go. Start digging, it is part of *getting ready*.

*By faith,* *"With God, all things are possible!"* (Matt. 19:26). He is in control of all. In our small way of thinking, we look at a life in a measure of years. One of our years equals one trip around the sun. If it is God's will, we might make it to 90 times around the sun or more. God measures time in eternity, He always was and always will be. Think about this, God is in control of how long it would take our Earth, the Sun, and our solar system to go around the Milky Way galaxy. Scientists estimate it would take 230 million years — that trip is called a cosmic year. That makes me scratch my balding head. He even knows how many hairs I have left. (This reference can be found in Matthew 10:30.)

He knows everything about us and about the universe, not just the *little* Milky Way galaxy. God wants us to know that He is real. *By faith* He wants us to know how He loves each of us more than we will ever understand. *"Ever since the world was created, people have seen the earth and sky. Through*

*everything God made, they can clearly see his invisible qualities —
His eternal power and divine nature. So they have no excuse for
not knowing God"* (Rom. 1:20).

How far away is the Kingdom of God? It is as close as
*your faith. "For God so loved the World that He gave His only
begotten Son, that whoever believes in Him should not perish but
have everlasting life"* (Jn. 3:16). Jesus spoke these words to the
Pharisee named Nicodemus after he asked. "How can a man
be born when he is old?" Nicodemus was listening with his
head (in the physical realm). But to be born from above, he
had to listen with his heart (in the spiritual realm).

In the section that follows, I really had to dig into my
study Bible to capture the essence of what I learned about
*regeneration.* This goldmine is called the New Geneva Study
Bible, and it was given to me by a good friend named Bill
Hinson. When he gave it to me, I was still a baby Christian,
about twenty years ago. At that point in my Christian walk,
it was like giving a 16-year-old student driver the keys to a
Formula One race car. Bill's gift of this Study Bible helped
me to quickly understand how the books and scriptures are
connected, and they all point to our Lord and Savior.

Being born again in a new birth or *regeneration* is an act
that only God can perform in which He renews the human
heart. God acts at the origin and deepest point of the human
person. This means there is no preparation nor a preceding
temperament in a sinner that requests a new life given by
God. This new birth is necessary because all descendants of
Adam and Eve have inherited their sin, and this sin keeps
us separated from God. *Regeneration* is the free gift of God's
grace. It is immediate and supernatural through the work of
the Holy Spirit. It awakens us from spiritual death to everlasting life. God has done His part by giving us His Son. It is
our responsibility to become born again *by faith* in Jesus. The

fruit of regeneration is faith. Regeneration comes before faith. And without faith, it is impossible to please God.

You probably have heard of how people are categorized into groups based on when they were born.[13]

| Generation name | Births start | Birth ends |
|---|---|---|
| The lost generation, or generation of 1914 | 1890 | 1915 |
| The interbellum generation | 1901 | 1913 |
| The greatest generation | 1910 | 1924 |
| The silent generation | 1925 | 1945 |
| Baby boomers | 1946 | 1964 |
| Generation X (baby bust) | 1965 | 1979 |
| Xennials | 1975 | 1985 |
| Millennials / generation Y / generation next | 1980 | 1994 |
| iGeneration / Generation z | 1995 | 2012 |
| Generation alpha | 2013 | 2025 |

What we need is an overlapping, all-inclusive generation called the free generation or *FreGeneration*. Free is good, freedom to be vocal about what we believe. Free to believe in the truth that will set us free. We are no longer chasing perfection because He loves us just the way we are. We have His love so we can go ahead and be who He made us to be. It changes everything: no more guilt, no more shame; He took it all away!

It is based on regeneration or being born again in Christ. Part of this truth is knowing what we are living life for, that is: *"to love the Lord your God with all your heart and with all your soul and with all your mind. Love your neighbor as yourself"* (Matt. 22:37–39). Please understand, *we are not human beings having a spiritual experience but spiritual beings having a human experience*. Based on these convictions, choosing regeneration will determine where we will end up for eternity.

FreGeneration is the generation group I want to be associated with because it won't be too much longer before the Uppertaker (rapture) or undertaker (death) will take us from this earth. Join the army of the FreGeneration and accept the free gift of salvation. Then go tell others the Good News by being vocal about what we believe.

**Are you set to go to Heaven?**

**Golden Step #11: By faith, Jesus gave us the right to become children of God.**

# CHAPTER 12

## HUMBLE BEAST

"I was senseless and ignorant; I was like a brute <u>beast</u> before you" (Ps. 73:22).

Part of getting set to go to Heaven is to transform from a *brute beast* into a *humble beast* in Christ. This is not easy to do because of our human nature wants affirmation, recognition, and praise for all the things we have accomplished. Freedom comes when you acknowledge that it is only by following God's plan that you have accomplished anything. One of your best rewards comes from not looking for man's endorsement but living *only* for God's approval. The day you start thinking for yourself instead of just following the mainstream is the day you finally have freedom.

Note: The title for this chapter comes from a shirt that I saw someone wearing at the gym. You can find more information on their sports apparel at www.humblebeast-inchrist.com.

As a man thinks, so he is. Freedom is the space between your ears. Be different following what you truly believe. I believe in Jesus, so that's why I refer to myself as a humble beast in Christ. *"Let the one who boasts boast in the Lord"* (2 Cor. 10:17). Also, if you feel the need to boast, here is another scripture to examine: *"'But let the one who boasts boast about this: that they have the understanding to know Me, that I am the Lord, who exercises kindness, justice and righteousness on earth, for in these I delight,' declares the Lord"* (Jer. 9:24). If you want to *delight the Lord,* you can demonstrate that you are truly a humble beast by exercising kindness, justice, and righteousness.

## Be Humble but Not Timid

I've read that Moses was the humblest man that ever lived. Do you think he would lose this distinction if he displayed it in the form of a trophy or certificate for all to see? Moses was humble probably because God had given him a second chance after he had killed an Egyptian. "He [Moses] saw an Egyptian beating a Hebrew, one of his own people. *Looking this way and that and seeing no one, he killed the Egyptian and hid him in the sand"* (Ex. 2:11–12). This death made Moses flee because the Pharaoh wanted to kill him after he knew of the murder. It was all in God's plan. You can find this story in Exodus Chapter 2. Moses then had an encounter with God via a conversation with a burning bush. He had to follow God's direction, and he became a *humble beast.* From that moment, Moses had to focus on the eternal rather than things of this earth. "Set your mind on things above, not on earthly things" (Col. 3:2). Give God control of your life, and He will equip you with what you need to fulfill His plan.

Back in 2008, I was serving in my position as postmaster of Odessa, Texas. A friend of mine who happened to be the district manager in Los Angeles called me to offer me an opportunity. He asked me to take on an assignment as maintenance manager for the Los Angeles processing and distribution center. It is the largest single-story mail processing facility in the world. When I told him, "But I don't have a background in maintenance," he responded with, "You're an excellent leader with great people skills, and that's what we need right now." He needed me there as soon as possible, so I left for Los Angeles on July 24, 2008, on Irma's birthday.

My new assignment came with the most responsibility I had ever experienced in my postal career, including assignments as processing manager in Oklahoma City, Oklahoma, and Little Rock, Arkansas. When I first walked the floor of this million-square-foot facility, I looked at it from one end to the other and thought I could see the curvature of the earth's horizon. It was huge!

During a staff meeting on July 29, five days after my assignment began, an earthquake rocked Los Angeles. There were about a dozen managers sitting around an oblong executive table. We all went under the table, and it felt like I was on a tilt-a-whirl. My thought was the ceiling was about to fall on us. After several seconds, the shaking, rattling, and rolling stopped. The district manager announced that everyone should evacuate the building. Some of the other managers ran out of the room; I stayed behind with my new boss. In just a short while, he received a call on his radio (walkie-talkie) advising him the employees did not want to reenter the building as it looked like some sky lights at the entrance had shifted. They were worried that the roof was unstable and the large acrylic windows would fall.

The district manager told me to go check it out and determine whether we could resume mail processing operations. I left his office with my mind spinning and thinking, "How the heck am I going to assess the damage caused by this stupid earthquake?" It was a long, lonely walk to the main entrance. As I looked through the skylights, I focused on God and asked Him to give me the wisdom to figure this out. The idea came into my head to have a couple of custodians go on top of the roof with a water hose. I instructed them to spray lots of water on the skylights from the topside. Underneath, I waited to see if there was any leakage. After several minutes with no water leaking through, I proclaimed the building safe to reenter. My new boss laughed when I told him how I determined it was safe to enter the building. He called it Chicano ingenuity. I give God the glory and call it a form of *shekinah* revelation. Note: the word *shekinah* does not appear in the Bible. It is a form of Hebrew that literally means, "He caused to dwell." Thank you, Lord, for providing my earthquake assessment ability that helped me as I was not equipped to make this call on my own.

My assignment in Los Angeles was challenging and through God's help, I was able to motivate a large workforce to work as a team. Below is a picture of a mural that was painted in the maintenance department. The other blessing that came with this assignment was Irma and I were blessed by worshipping three years at Angeles Temple. Our faith increased, and we received strength from hearing the Word from Pastor Matthew Barnett and many testimonies of second chances.

One of my best friends, Dean Williams, sent me the picture of the mural in the maintenance department at the Los Angeles mail processing center. As a true instigator, he added a red laser line to the picture to demonstrate how my replica stood taller than the boss's replica. But in reality, I was just a humble beast, a servant to the Lord.

Mural in the maintenance department at the Los Angeles Mail
Processing Center.

Let's get back to examining Moses and how God equipped
him. First, he was raised by the Pharaoh's daughter when
she felt sorry for the baby (Moses) in a basket among the
reeds along the banks of the Nile River. The name Moses
sounds like the Hebrew expression for *draw out*. The
Pharaoh's daughter *"named him Moses saying, 'I drew him out
of water'"* (Ex. 2:10). As a result, Moses and his biological
mother lived in the Pharaoh's household. Why did Moses's
biological mother get to go along? Well, because that was
God's plan. You see, when the Pharaoh's daughter needed
a Hebrew woman to nurse her adopted son, her sister just
happened to pick Moses's mother, and she was even paid
to nurse her own baby. Moses was raised having the best
of the Egyptian world. I wonder if he learned to *walk like an
Egyptian*. (Hopefully, you have heard of that song.) He was

155

probably trained in self-defense, and that may have aided him when he killed the Egyptian that was beating a Hebrew.

God also provided Moses with some signs so he could go face the Pharaoh. Moses's staff when thrown on the ground became a snake, and his hand became leprous when he put it in his cloak and pulled it out. He could then put it back in his cloak and pulled it out restored. Moses was still reluctant to go face the Pharaoh. Moses knew he had a problem with stuttering. I guess it would make me stutter too if God began a conversation with me via a burning bush. Moses pointed out, *"O Lord, I have never been eloquent...but I am slow of speech and slow of tongue"* (Ex. 4:10). As this conversation continues, *"So the Lord said to him, 'Who has made a man's mouth? Or who makes the mute, the deaf, the seeing or the blind? Have not I, the Lord?'"* (Ex. 4:11–12). But Moses said, *"O my Lord please send by the hand of whomever else You may send."* So the <u>anger</u> of the Lord was <u>kindled</u> against Moses ..." So God chooses Aaron, Moses's brother, who was a Levite and able to speak well. God also tells Moses that Aaron is on his way to meet up with him.

**Bonus Note on Aaron:** He was three years older than Moses and therefore was spared as only newborn infant boys were being thrown into Nile during the time when Moses was born. (See Exodus 1:15–22.)

Anyway, God selected Moses's brother Aaron to do the talking. So together they went to face the Pharaoh to bring the Israelites out of captivity; they were *humble* but not *timid*. They were equipped with miraculous signs, and they knew God was for them. God further demonstrated his power when He sent 10 plagues against Egypt. He directly attacked the gods and symbols that the Egyptians worshipped to display His Glory. God multiplied His signs and wonders in the land of Egypt so the Egyptians might know He is the Lord.

I encourage you to dig into your Bible; this is part of *getting set* to go to Heaven. Read about what God's name is: I AM WHO I AM. He is Elohim, the Lord God of our fathers, the God of Abraham, the God of Isaac, and the God of Jacob. He is the same, yesterday, today, and forever.

Take time to read the detail in the parting of the Red Sea miracle and how God separated the Israelites from the Egyptians. The entire story of the Red Sea crossing is found in Chapter 14 of Exodus. Take time to examine the details in this chapter; *it will increase your faith*. Here is a portion, but it will be up to you to *read the entire story*.

*"The Egyptians pursued them, and all Pharaoh's horses and chariots and horsemen followed them into the seas. During the last watch of the night the Lord looked down from the pillar of fire and cloud at the Egyptian army and threw it into confusion. He made the wheels of their chariots come off so they had difficulty driving…"* (Ex. 14:24–25).

When God is for you, who can be against you? Go out and tell others about Him with confidence because *"For the Lord your God is the one who goes with you to fight for you against your enemies to give your victory"* (Deut. 20:4).

Remember, when God gives you an assignment, He will also equip you with what you need to finish it. God has your back, so go forward in confidence. Like my brother in Christ Pastor Joel Perales would say, "Get on your knees and come out fighting."

## Be Strong but Not Rude

In October 2019, I had an encounter with a homeless man that gave me a new perspective on life. He was difficult to deal with as he was upset with his current circumstances. He was aggressive toward me, and I had to use self-control to engage with him so I could learn a life lesson. Here is an excerpt from *Broken Walk: Searching for Wisdom*:

It was a morning filled with wonder as we prepared for going into skid row in the downtown area of Los Angeles. We wore Dream City shirts which are recognized by the homeless as "good guy" shirts. We had to be careful where we stepped because there were spots with puddles and no clouds in the sky. My eyes felt sympathy as we stopped and prayed for various individuals. I am thankful God gave me the boldness to pray without fear as it felt odd to have someone who is homeless clinging to me with their cheek pressed to mine. Somehow that morning my Spanish received a spiritual change of sparkplugs. I offered hope to several who preferred to converse in the first language I learned. We were giving away popcorn and water. Many of the homeless wanted only water and tried to convince us to give them two waters and no popcorn. As much as I hated to, I had to ration the water so we could spread the blessing to as many as we could. My job was to pull the water wagon and I had to maneuver it off the sometimes-dilapidated sidewalk. Our walk-through skid row ended at a park where there was a basketball court and several areas to sit. Approaching the park there was a faint smell of marijuana.

Since I was pulling the water cart on the street, I was able to notice a man standing next to a port-a-john just outside of the park on the edge of the sidewalk. He looked somewhat out of place as he wore a reflective vest like a person working for a maintenance company. I could not tell if he was one of the homeless, so I offered him my personal bag of popcorn that I was saving for myself to keep my energy level up.

He looked surprised and remarked, "No one from your group ever talks to me because they don't think I'm homeless. You are the first to offer me something!"

I told him, "Well that's probably because you have that nice vest on and look like a park maintenance worker." He promptly lifted his vest to display his overused shirt and pants that needed a couple of wash cycles.

He said, "I am homeless too!" with a faint Jamaican accent.

He told me his name was Ceven, and I asked if it was spelled like the number seven. He seemed annoyed and responded, "No! C-E-V-E-N" as he spelled it out. He said he wished people would get it right. I quickly changed the subject as I did not want to engage in a meaningless debate over the spelling of Ceven versus seven. *He was very aggressive, and I felt like he wanted to beat me up.*

I asked him, "What do you do here?"

He said, "God gave me the assignment to keep this bathroom clean even though I don't get paid. I'm here every day and clean up mess after mess." He told me how much he hated it but God gave him the assignment and told him to do it.

I was stunned by this and told him about the Dream Center. He said he had never heard of it. I pointed the leaders in the group that could offer him more information as I was only in Los Angeles for a week.

He seemed interested but told me, "None of dem talk to me."

I told him that I was 100 percent sure they would listen to him if he approached them. My prayer is this homeless servant of the homeless has gotten the help he needs.

I cried in my bunk bed that night when I realized I now knew what true humility was. My mind pondered, how can a person who is homeless devote his life to cleaning a public port-a-john on skid row? The answer was humility and obedience. God let me know, right then, that I needed more of it. Have you ever cried to the point where tears rolled into your ears?

I'm glad that God allowed me to be *strong* while not responding with *rudeness* that day in October 2019. In my former self, I would have been rude to Ceven and put him in my rearview mirror. I found out my purpose for the remainder of my life at the end of my tears. My last days on earth will be full of gratitude when I write or speak of His Goodness. My prayer is to be strong when I boast in Him. May God give me the ability to roar like a lion about Him but never in a rude manner.

## Be Kind but Not Weak

Look at the example provided by Jesus when the Pharisees laid a plan to trap Him in His words.

*The Pharisees asked him the question, "Tell us then, what is your opinion? Is it right to pay the imperial tax to Caesar or not?" But Jesus, knowing their evil intent said, "You hypocrites, why are you trying to trap me? Show me the coin used for paying the tax." They brought Him a denarius, and he asked them, "Whose image is this? And whose inscription?"*

*"Caesar's," they replied.*

*Then He said to them, "So give to Caesar what is Caesar's and to God what is God's." When they heard this, they were amazed. So they left Him and went away"* (Matt. 22:17-22)

Jesus was *kind* but not *weak* in His response. He could have easily made the Pharisees choke to death on those very coins or their words of evil intent.

We must learn how to be more like Him and choose words carefully. We must remain kind when others are testing us without being weak in our words or conviction. There are times when you must stand for what you believe instead of being silent. Silence is a form of agreement, especially in the areas of religion and politics. These are two areas my father-in-law (RIP, Speedy) told me we should never engage in. My conviction, when it comes to protecting the children and the unborn, leads me to be vocal. When I am in a discussion with someone who has an opposite opinion, it is best to invoke: "We need to agree to disagree and move on." That's part of getting into the humble beast mode.

## Be Proud but Not Arrogant

As followers of Christ, we should take pride that we are the salt of the earth and the light of the world. We need to be seasoned as we speak the Word of God to correct, rebuke, and encourage with great patience and careful instruction. Way back in the summer of 1967, I worked during a youth camp at Our Lady of Fatima. There was a nun who supervised my friend Rosario and me. She loved to tell us in a harsh manner, "You're not worth your salt!" The way she said it was distasteful and hurtful. We did not like helping her on any projects because it seemed like we could not do anything that pleased her. It would have been better if she had used more patience and given us careful instruction. On the way home, Rosario and I would shrug it off by telling each other, "You ain't worth your salt!" The scripture in Matthew 4:13 reads, *"You are the salt of the earth. But if the salt loses its saltiness, how can it be made salty again. It is no longer good for anything, except to be thrown out and trampled by men."* In my opinion, she had lost her saltiness by being *proud* and *arrogant*.

Our behavior and how we treat others should reflect the image of Jesus living inside of us. We should be like a lighthouse that can help navigate lost souls through rugged water in times of darkness. We need to shine bright so others want to walk with us toward Heaven. I'm thankful that the Word of God is a lamp to our feet. Here is a promise that will put some bounce in your step. *"But if we walk in the light, as He is in the Light, we have fellowship with one another, and the blood of Jesus,*

*His Son, purifies us from all sin"* (1 Jn, 1:7). We should be *proud* to belong to the Body of Christ—never in *arrogance* or self-righteousness but only to shine for the glory of our Father alone.

There is a story found in Matthew 20:20-28. Please make time to look it up in your Bible. It is about James and John (sons of Zebedee), whose mother came to ask Jesus for a special favor. She requested that her sons could sit at Jesus's right and left when at His kingdom. Jesus asked James and John if they could "drink of His cup" that He was going to drink. In an *arrogant* manner, they responded that they could. They thought Jesus was setting up a kingdom on earth. Jesus told them the positions at the right and left of Him were not for Him to grant, but His Father would make this choice. Jesus continued to tell them whoever wants to become great must be ready to serve others first—just like He did. Jesus is the ultimate humble beast—proud to be the Son of the Father but never arrogant.

As the ultimate humble beast, Jesus is the Lion of Judah but also the Lamb of God. He loved us so much He gave His life for us. If the Roman soldiers could not have nailed Him to the Cross, He would have pounded those nails in by Himself. He did not want to do it, but He knew it had to be done. Shortly before He was arrested, he prayed in the Garden of Gethsemane. *"He fell to the ground and prayed that if possible the hour might pass Him. 'Abba, Father, everything is possible for you. Take this cup from Me. Yet not what I will, but what you will'"* (Mk. 14:35-36). In the true fashion of a humble beast He chose to sacrifice Himself for us. He humbled Himself to the Cross to pay for all our sins.

Jesus is the visible image of the invisible God. He is God's only begotten Son, the firstborn over all creation. In Him, all things were created in Heaven and on earth both visible and invisible. Jesus was made flesh so we could be reconciled to the Father. He made peace for us through His blood shed on the Cross—the Lamb of God who takes away the sin of the world.

Jesus showed us how to become a humble beast, He stepped out of Heaven and took on being a lowly human. *"And being found in appearance as a man, He humbled Himself by becoming obedient to death—even a death on a cross!"* (Phil. 2:8). By doing this He now sits at the right hand of the Father, and at the name of Jesus every knee will bow in Heaven and on earth.

We need to follow His example and humble ourselves for the good of others. *Getting into your humble beast mode is the best way to live your life!* Whatever we do while waiting to go to Heaven, whether in word or action, we do it as a representative of Christ. Just like Him we must give thanks to God the Father in everything so it brings Him glory.

Finally, *getting set* is living *"a life worthy of the Lord and please Him in every way: bearing fruit in every good work, growing in the knowledge of God, being strengthened with all power according to His glorious might so that you may have great endurance and patience, and giving joyful thanks to the Father, who has qualified you to share in the inheritance of His holy people in the Kingdom of the Light. For He has rescued us from the dominion of darkness and brought us into the Kingdom of the Son He loves, in whom we have redemption, the forgiveness of sins"* (Col. 1:10–14).

**Golden Step #12: Imitate Jesus to become a humble beast in Christ.**

# CHAPTER 13

## WORDS OF WISDOM

*"My mouth will speak <u>words of wisdom</u>; the meditation of my heart will give you understanding"* (Ps. 49:3).

Part of our *getting set* to go to Heaven is to help others by offering them words of *affirmation, encouragement,* and *wisdom*. Whenever we have the opportunity, we need to speak life. *"The tongue has the power of life and death and those who love it will eat of its fruit"* (Prov. 18:21). There is vast meaning in this verse; simply put, we must be careful with our words because they can do good or harm. What you say with your words could come back to bless you or hurt you. Physical bruises go away, but hateful words remain with us always and echo in our memory. If you use harsh words, you will probably get some in return. If you offer words to affirm, encourage, and give advice, you may get them back when you need it most. Remember, out of the abundance of the heart, the mouth speaks. Make sure your words are seasoned in love and your conversation is full of grace. *You are what you think and have in your heart; you will get back what you speak.*

## Words of Affirmation

Parents sometimes name their children to affirm a course in life they hope their child will take. One of my former co-workers is named Governor and another Plumber. I've known of kids from south of the border to be named Freedom and America. One of my favorites is Christian and I also enjoyed working at the post office with a young lady named Charisma. All young boys and girls need a boost of affirmation so they can gain confidence as they figure out their call in life. I certainly needed it back then, and my ears still gobble it up even as an old dude.

There was a teacher who enhanced my skills in leadership by appointing me as the president of our fifth-grade class at Jackson Elementary school back in 1962. Early in the school year, she announced to my classmates my appointment. There were no campaign promises, ballot counting, or voting. She affirmed my appointment as president, and that was that. My friends Manuel Aguirre, Genevie Iniguez, and Susie Camacho were among those classmates. This happened just before our country lost its innocence; it was a year before President Kennedy was assassinated. It was before civil rights rioting and the killing of Martin Luther King Jr. and Robert Kennedy. As fifth graders we were in our wonder years and enjoying our way of life in those good old days.

Here is an excerpt from my first book, *Barrio Walk*:

During the fifth grade, there was a teacher who inspired me to learn and it was the first time I received a straight A report card. Miss McDowell appointed me as the class president and told my classmates I was in charge if she had to step away from the classroom. Our classroom was a cottage that was detached from the main school building. One of my primary duties was to lock the cottage when we left and open the door after lunch and recess. It felt good to hold the small American flag as I led my classmates in reciting the Pledge of Allegiance as we began our school day. *"Blessed is the Nation whose God is the Lord"* (Psalm 33:12).

Some of the kids called me teacher's pet, but as the year went on, they did not mind me being in charge when Miss McDowell stepped away. There was a really cute girl named Susan who had an interest in me. Even though she looked like Halle Berry, my agenda did not include girlfriends. During the summer before fifth grade, we (Sherman Street boys) formed a small club named the Monster club, and our first rule was no girls allowed. We had weekly meetings and collected dues that we hid in a hole inside my dad's *cuartito* (small shack). Larry Eagleman designed our own club membership card as we pondered how we would help our country beat the Russians to the moon.

My fifth-grade teacher's birthday was on February 14, which is also Arizona Statehood Day. On that special day, it is also Cupid's day to shoot arrows. As the class prez, I was able to organize a surprise party where we brought in goodies and a small 45 rpm phonograph. The principal helped us keeping Miss McDowell away from the cottage long enough that afternoon for a surprise birthday celebration. She was touched to the point of tears, and we had a blast. Before the party we rearranged our desks so we could have a limbo contest. "How low can you go?" For you youngsters, that's a lyric from that limbo song. We also had fun dancing to a new song by Chubby Checker called "The Twist." It was a moment that has stayed engrained in the walls of my memory bank, and when I hear that song, I always dance inside just like back then. What song makes you dance?

It was awesome because Miss McDowell said it, and just like that, I was president the entire school year and did not get impeached.

## Beautiful Are the feet

Going back almost twenty years, Irma and I attended a marriage conference where one of the speakers invited couples to approach her when she had finished speaking. When we reached the area just in front of her, she surprised me when she dropped to her knees and touched our feet. She quoted a scripture that I was not familiar with at that time. From Isaiah 52:7, *"How beautiful on the mountain are the feet of those who bring good news, who proclaim peace, who bring good tidings and who proclaim salvation!"* She went on to say that we would teach the good news to many. At the time, I had no idea what she was talking about and was slightly embarrassed by her being at our feet. Today, I thank this woman of God who spoke words of affirmation into our lives.

In October 2016, my cousin Cathy Quihuiz Leyva and her husband, Gilbert, visited us in Texas. They are pastors at a church in California. The four of us went to visit our son Anthony in San Antonio. Anthony and Analuisa had recently been blessed by God with their firstborn son they named Samuel Colt. (He has the stamina of a young pony as he constantly runs.) My cousin Cathy held Samuel and spoke *words of affirmation* in his two-week old life. She said he would grow up to become a man of God.

Well, it's working! Yesterday, Samuel, who is now 4 and a half years old, told me his daddy cut his hand, but it was going to be okay because he prayed for it. His words caught me off guard, but I did ask him to show me how he prayed for it. He grabbed Anthony's hand and closed his small eyelids. Samuel said, "Father God, please heal my daddy's hand in Jesus's name." He then kissed Anthony's hand and said he knew his daddy's cut would heal. As he ran off to go find some more caterpillars, I thanked God with misty eyes for my cousin Cathy's words of affirmation.

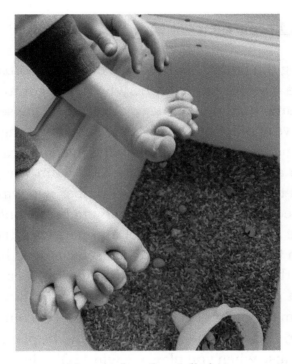

My grandson Samuel's feet.
May they one day bring the Good News to many.

The greatest words of affirmation from God that I have read in the Bible are: "*… that whoever believes in Him should not perish but have everlasting life.*" It doesn't get any clearer or simpler than that. Our problem as humans is we complicate things by making it about us. We want to earn our way into Heaven through our prayers, our fasting, our giving to the poor, lighting candles, saying novenas, rubbing buddhas, and good deeds. In Isaiah 64:6 it says, "*all our righteous acts* *are like filthy rags."* There is no way we can ever earn our way into Heaven. God loved us so much He gave us Jesus. It was our Savior *only* that paid for our sins. He is the *only* way to the Father. Jesus did His part when He affirmed, *"It is finished."*

## Words of Encouragement

During the Friday Night Lights of Texas football season, there was a senior named Moe who never got to play in a varsity game until one of the final games of the season. He was always at practice, full of desire and chomping at the bit to get some live game action. Finally, the game came when Moe was able to enter the game. Our team was winning 44-3, and the coach called Moe's number. He was thrilled. He stopped and waved back at his mom before entering the game. He also forgot his helmet and had to hurry back to the bench to retrieve it before the coach changed his mind.

After the victory, Moe was grinning from ear to ear. I made it a point to go up to him and tell him how proud I was of him for always being ready to play. I encouraged him by saying, "If I were the coach, you would be playing all the time. Because when you play, we win 44-3!" He thanked me profusely before he joined his teammates in celebration.

Those *words of encouragement* did not cost me anything and acknowledged Moe's hard work and dedication. Take time to encourage someone — you do not know what they might be going through.

The best time to offer encouragement is when someone is sick and perhaps dying. Don't just say. "I'll pray for you." Stop right then and say a prayer with them. It feels good to the receiver when someone says, "I'll pray for you," but it feels way better to them when they actually hear your prayer. I can still remember my Tia Tillie (RIP) praying for me as I was leaving Arizona in 1990. It is my belief that I'm still covered by a hedge of protection she sent with me off with that day.

Every day is a step closer to our own death on earth. Irma and I make it a habit to say nightly, "If I don't see you in the morning, I'll see you up there." We do not know when the Lord will take us, so we *encourage* each other with our faith of meeting in Heaven. I usually end our night by talking about what I will eat for breakfast; those are *words of hope*. Our days are not guaranteed and *"You (we) are a mist that appears for a little while and then vanishes"* (Jm. 4:14). Life is short, and the days seem to go by faster as you get older except when you are waiting for the next stimulus check.

About two months before my father passed away in 2002, I used the words of encouragement that Paul wrote in 1 Thessalonians 4:16-18 as I was saying goodbye to my father. *"For the Lord Himself will descend from Heaven with a shout, with the voice of an archangel, and with the trumpet of God. And the dead in Christ will rise first. Then we who are alive and remain shall be caught up together with them in the clouds to meet the Lord in the air. And thus, we shall always be with the Lord. Therefore* comfort *one another with these words.*

Below is an excerpt from my second book *Broken Walk*:

**The Last Look**–As clearly as the sun is bright, my dad's last look into my eyes still illuminates like a shiny gold coin in the memory bank of my mind. About six weeks before my father "jumped" into Jesus's arms, we touched foreheads, and I told him, "If I don't see you again, I'll see you up there." We both sadly smiled because we knew this was our goodbye. He had an incredible look of love that I saw with blurry vision because of my tears. Many people do not get a chance to say goodbye because of death or divorce.

Maybe the farewell has been stolen by Alzheimer's or a brain injury. Life is unpredictable and sometimes tragic. That is why we must forgive and show kindness to those closest to you. Always keep love in your heart and peace in your soul. It is difficult to say goodbye, but it is less troublesome when you can look back without regrets or unresolved issues. Our time on earth is not guaranteed.

Use the words of Paul in 1 Thessalonians Chapter 4 to encourage someone who is nearing death. Read the words to them to booster their faith, and it will also enhance yours.

## Words of Wisdom to Live By

The best two words of wisdom I can offer are: <u>Trust God.</u> No matter what happens, in the end, God wins. When God is for you, it doesn't matter who or what comes against you. *"...neither death nor life, nor angels nor principalities nor powers, nor things present nor things to come, nor height nor depth nor any other created thing, shall be able to separate us from the love of God which is in Christ Jesus our Lord"* (Rom. 8:38). His presence fills every place on earth and everywhere on the universe. He occupies that enormous space on the other side of the sun to the tiniest space in your heart, all at the same time. Wow! All glory, honor, and trust to our Father in Heaven.

As a young man, I remember taking my first taxi ride from Dominguez Seminary to my tio Ralph's place of employment. Being 15 years old, I asked the cab driver if he liked his job. He forcefully told me, "Look, kid, if you don't want a loser job like this, stay in school and get a degree!" A few years later, an elderly man that I met at Carlito's Market gave me this advice, "This is what you want from life, get a job where you work very little and get paid a lot." I asked him if that worked for him, and he said, "That doesn't matter because my life is almost over." My co-workers and I would say he was old as the hills and twice as dusty. Later in my career even though I was paid well, with all the hours I put in, I was making less than minimum wage. The work was strenuous mentally, and it took its toll on my family life and health.

The *words of wisdom to live by* I offer to a young person is to find a job they absolutely love. Then your work ethics should follow the wise words found in Colossians 3:23. *"Whatever you do, work at it with all your heart, as working for the Lord, not human masters."* Here is Irma's favorite verse that contains some sound *words of wisdom*. *"Make it your ambition to lead a quiet life: You should mind your own business and work with your hands...so that your daily life may win the respect of outsiders and so that you will not be dependent on anybody"* (1 Thess. 4:11–12).

As we get older and our physical strength decreases, wisdom should increase if you are spending time in the Word of God. Here are two more *words of wisdom to live by* to help you in getting set to go to Heaven: <u>Stop worrying.</u> God is in control, and He has a better plan for your life than you do. If He can change night into day, He can fix anything you are facing. All worrying does is it makes you carry tomorrow's workload using today's strength. It does not empty tomorrow's burdens. It just empties the strength you have today. Part of the peace in knowing you are going to Heaven is chilling knowing that God whispers daily, "I got this!"

He sent His Son to pay the price of our sins by His death on the Cross. His Son resurrected and sits at the right Hand of our Father. That's the *Good News*.

The *Better News* is:

- He is coming again – John 21:22–24;
- He is in Heaven praying for us – Hebrews 7:25;
- He is preparing a place for us – John 14:1–3.

The *Bestest News* while we *get set to go to Heaven* is: We will be with Him soon.

## The Armor of God

While *getting set* to go to Heaven, it is important to put on the whole armor of God every day. This will allow us to withstand whatever evil may come at us and be able to stand. Read about this armor in the book of Ephesians 6:10–18. It includes the following that will make you feel like a super-hero. You will be armed with the following:

❖ The helmet of salvation – *"And there is <u>salvation</u> in no one else"* (Acts 4:12).

❖ The shield of faith – *"Now <u>faith</u> is the substance of things hoped for, the evidence of things not seen."* (Heb. 11:1);

❖ The breastplate of righteousness – *"He made Him who knew no sin to be sin on our behalf, so we might become the <u>righteousness</u> of God in Him"* (2 Cor. 5:21);

❖ The belt of truth – *"Buy the truth and do not sell it – wisdom, instruction and insight as well"* (Prov. 23:23);

❖ The sword of the spirit – *For the word of God is quick and powerful and sharper than any two-edged <u>sword</u>, piercing even to the division of soul and spirit, and joints and marrow, and is a discerner of thoughts and intents of the heart"* (Heb. 4:12);

❖ Feet prepared with the Gospel of peace – *"How beautiful are the <u>feet</u> of them that preach the <u>gospel of peace</u> and bring glad tidings of good things"* (Rom. 10:15).

You can also *get set* for your Golden Walk by studying in Ephesians chapter 4 that will tell you how to be an imitator of God by walking in love, light, and wisdom.

During the last two years, I started a Facebook page called Wisdom United that has grown to more than 2,700 followers. The numerous postings include a picture to reinforce the message. Below are a few of the posts that received the most likes:

• If you want to know someone's mind, listen to their words. If you want to know someone's heart, watch their actions.

• Feed your Faith, and your fears will starve to death.

• Birds of a feather will one day fly to Heaven together.

• Sometimes good things fall apart so better things can fall together.

• We can't always control our circumstances, but we can control our attitude.

• Keep smiling, be generous, and spread joy. Let your words heal and not wound.

• Ask yourself what is really important; then have the wisdom and courage to build your life around that answer.

- Hope is the thing with feathers that perches in the soul and sings the tunes without the words — and never stops (Emily Dickinson).

- Keep a song in your heart, a smile on your face, and praise him always.

- Be kind to the unkind...That's how God treats us.

- Walk in a manner that glorifies God.

- The Bible is meant to be bread for daily use, not cake for special occasions.

- Better to have friends that can help you pray through a mess than having friends that will keep you in a mess.

- Be a beacon of peace and grace displayed by a smile on your face. No matter what you are facing today, shine for Jesus, the storm will go away.

- When hate is loud, love must be louder.

- Someone somewhere is depending on you to do what God has called you to do.

- Words kill, words give life; they're either poison or fruit — You choose!

In the words of Joyce Meyer,[14] "*Enjoy where you are on your way to where you are going.*" Words are like keys, and if you choose them correctly, they can open any heart or door of opportunity. They can also cause a lifetime of damage or a broken relationship in a moment of anger. When you are making necessary adjustments to correct yourself, use your head. When living in peace with those around you, choose words that come from your heart. Always stay in the spirit of love, and if necessary, walk away and pray about it. This will give you the moment you need to search your heart for your next words.

Every day is a new beginning, every month a new paragraph, and every year adds a chapter. Fill your life book with words of *affirmation, encouragement, and wisdom.* At the end of your book, you will be remembered by the *words of wisdom* you gave to those you love. (Whoever is reading this — that's *you.*) We love because He loved us first.

**Golden Step #13: Speak life into others with words of affirmation, encouragement, and wisdom.**

# PART THREE – LET'S GO

# CHAPTER 14

## DO NOT FEAR

*"For I am the Lord your God who takes hold of your right hand and says to you, <u>Do not fear</u>; I will help you"* (Isa. 41:13).

So here we are in the final section of Golden Walk. What will Heaven be like? It's going to be infinitely more beautiful and serene than anywhere you have been on earth. My encouragement to you about Heaven is beyond my capacity to describe what it will look and be like.

It is like explaining to a mustard seed before planting it into the ground that one day it will be an enormous tree. The seed cannot understand how it will transform into many branches providing shade and a place for birds to build their nest. Or it is like telling a caterpillar to keep spinning its cocoon because one day it will transform into a beautiful butterfly of many colors. The caterpillar has no concept about the freedom to stop crawling and gaining new ability to fly.

Eternity is an enormous concept that is difficult to grasp in our limited way of thinking. What will it be like? Will we get bored and run out of things to do? What will eternity with God be like? God invented time, and He exists outside of it. He was around time before time; He stays ahead of time.

He always was and always will be. *"Your throne was established long ago; You are from all eternity"* (Ps. 93:2).

For now, we must trust God. His Word tells throughout the Bible what Heaven will be. In 2 Corinthians 2:9, it says, *"However, as it is written: 'What no eye has seen, what no ear has heard, and what no mind has conceived' – the things God has prepared for those who love Him.* The word of God says it. Relax, it's gonna be good!

## Facing Death

When I get to the point of facing death, I want to have no fear just like my spiritual grandma. When I was working in Odessa, Texas, I had the privilege of meeting Grandma Thelma. She was our church grandmother, and we became remarkably close. She was just over ninety years old, and I loved talking with her. She told me, "Son, when the rapture comes, I will rise from my grave and do somersaults into Heaven!" She had dark blue eyes that would twinkle when she talked about going to Heaven. She would get animated and excited when talking about going to Heaven. She had no fear, whatsoever, about death because she knew where she was going. At times she was childlike as she would ask me privately if someone was white or of another nationality. She said she was color-blind and could not distinguish skin tones. *I wish we were all that way.*

At the National Day of Prayer luncheon, we sat together, and she proudly told everyone I was the postmaster. As the luncheon went on, she saw me engaged in a conversation with Larry, the mayor. When I got back to the table, she told me she wanted to meet the mayor. I brought Larry over and said, "Mayor, this is my grandmother." Larry shook her hand and said, "Pleased to meet you." Grandma shook his hand and said, "He's not really my grandson!" The mayor chuckled.

After this incident when a I saw grandma at church, I teased her by telling her I could not believe she dissed me in front of the mayor. Unfortunately, Grandma caught pneumonia shortly after a few weeks, and I went to see her at the hospital. She was in bad shape and only had a few more hours to live. When she saw me, she pulled her oxygen mask off and asked me to forgive her for disowning me in front of the mayor. I burst into tears and told her, "Grandma, please put your oxygen mask back on, I was only kidding!" Karma had paid me back for overdoing my playful teasing. When she saw I was shook up, she comforted me with the most tender look I have ever seen and caressed my head. That was the last time I saw Grandma Thelma on earth as I will see her again in Heaven. She looked angelic, tranquil, and unafraid. As we left her room, she confidently smiled as she knew her time was almost over. Her spirit left the room in a few hours. She became absent from her body and instantly present with the Lord. Jesus was glad to see her as this is confirmed by the following scripture. *"Precious in the eyes of the Lord are the deaths of His Saints"* (Ps. 116:15).

I long to be just like Grandma Thelma at my moment of death. It will be the best reward ever to look into those precious eyes of the Lord and hear the words, "Well done!"

## Have No Fear — Jesus Is Waiting for Us

Take comfort in knowing that Jesus has gone before us to prepare a place for us. He consoled His apostles with this promise: *"Let not your heart be troubled; you believe in God, believe also in Me. In My Father's House are many mansions; if it were not so, I would have told you. I go and prepare a place for you. And if I go and prepare a place for you, I will come again and receive you to Myself; that where I am, there you may be also"* (Jn. 14:1–3).

First, we must believe in God and that Jesus is God in unity with the Holy Spirit. *"I and the Father are one"* (Jn. 10:30). Then comes the <u>Good News</u>: God sent His Son because He loves us so much. His Son Jesus died for us and rose from the dead. Jesus loves us so much He sent the Holy Spirit to be with us on earth to guide us. On the day of Pentecost, the Apostles were all together when a violent wind came from Heaven and filled the house. *"All of them were filled with the Holy Spirit and began to speak in other tongues as the Spirit enabled them"* (Acts 2:4).

Remember, in the book of John Chapter 14, Jesus did not say these words during a time when He was telling stories through parables or as children gathered around him. He made these promises as he was saying goodbye to his twelve disciples. He told them about His imminent crucifixion. His friends were frightened, so to comfort them His words were, *"Let not your heart be troubled."* What an incredible Savior we have! At the most difficult time in His Life as He was facing the worst punishment ever, He still drew enough strength to comfort them. Instead of looking for sympathy, He thought of them. All praise and Glory to God the Father, His Son Jesus, and the Holy Spirit.

Our <u>Best News ever</u>: We will be with Him soon, so there is *no* need to *fear*. He will be there to comfort us and welcome us Home.

## No More

Please keep an open mind as you read these next two segments of this chapter. In parts of this reading, there are scriptures to reinforce what we can anticipate about Heaven. In other parts, it is my creative thinking just trying to expand our imagination.

When we get to Heaven it will be in a land of *no more* longing for a better place to live. We will finally be at our Home Sweet Home. *No more* searching for that perfect home that does not exist on earth for us. We always want more. There will be many rooms in our Father's House. The good thing for us old-timers is there will be *no more* forgetting why we entered a room in our House. *No more* losing my watch for the weekend, only to find it on Monday morning in my lunch box. It will be like that childhood home where you first experienced the love of family, the joy of Christmas, and mom's special cooking. Best of all, we get to see Jesus. There will be *no more* darkness in Heaven because we will receive light from the glory of God. *"The city (Heaven) had no need of the sun or the moon to shine in it, for the glory of God illuminated it. The Lamb is its light"* (Rev. 21:23).

There will be *no more* dementia or any other disease. *No more* worrying about COVID-19 and wearing masks. *No more* debate on the pros and cons of the vaccination. *No more* walking into the shower with my glasses on. *No more* aches and pains. Perhaps we can take a shower where we are drenched in liquid peace. Better yet, how about a bath in a pool of patience? The pond for our soul will be full of living water, and we will have *no more* thirst.

The sky's the limit when thinking about Heaven. There will be *no more* nightmares, our dreams will include millions of rainbows without even closing our eyes. *No more* physical limitations. Maybe I'll finally be able to run a 10K race under 50 minutes. Maybe I'll be able to challenge and beat a cheetah in a foot race for his bag of Cheetos. Will we be able to fly? It would be nice to visit an eagle's nest to offer the *eaglitos* (Tex-Mex for baby eagles) some food as long as it is not my fingers.

There will be *no more* fear. It would be wonderful to zipline from the moon to Camelback Mountain at the speed of light. My training days for one day getting surfing lessons will be *no more* because I'll be able to surf down Saturn's rings without getting wet. There will be *no more* choking on salt water when snorkeling. What if we can breathe underwater and see clearly without goggles? What if we can float so well underwater that it makes a jellyfish get jelly? (Jealous with pickle-colored eyes.) *No more* sound of complaining, confusion, despair, or the abrasion of different opinions. *No more* harsh words or name-calling. No more walking on eggshells because of a disagreement. *No more* having to remember passwords. *No more* death, *no more* tears, and *no more* hurt. *No more* of that gut-wrenching feeling when you watch your loved one being lowered into the ground.

There will be *no more* scars on our new bodies. I won't even have the small one on my left hand. The one I got from falling in 1958 on my way to Jackson School on a piece of glass near the railroad tracks. *The only scars you'll see in Heaven will belong to Jesus. When you see His Hands, Feet, and Side, you will then fully comprehend how much He suffered.* What if God replaces all the legs and arms of amputees? It will be wonderful to have *no more* knee pain nor ringing in my ears. There will be *no more* hunger as we gobble down *goodness* from the Tree of Life. No more running out of propane while cooking for company. There will be *no more* sorrow as we will get to jump up and down on a trampoline made from joy. *No more* empty love tank after we receive a kiss of kindness from our Savior. *No more* riding on that merry-go-round at the drive-in that was unsafe as a kid. The new ride will be on a roller coaster with a steering wheel called *self-control.*

*No more* sinking in sand; instead, we will be engulfed by the quicksand of His love. *No more* feeling of abandonment as we get wrapped in the *gentleness* of His security. *No more* discrimination because of skin color. *No more* violence, murder, and wars. *No more* crime, pollution, or corruption. Heaven is the safest place ever (Matt. 6:20).

*No more* doubts about Heaven being real — we will see it. Whatever God has for us In Heaven, our eyes will drool with delight. *"Eye has not seen, nor ear heard, nor have entered into the heart of man, the things which God has prepared for those who love Him"* (1 Cor. 9:9). Speaking of eyes, there will be *no more* tears. *"And God will wipe away every tear from their eyes"* (Rev. 7:17).

Have you ever heard of the legend of Apache tears? According to this legend, in 1875 the US Army found a secret path up a cliff (now called Apache Mountain Leap) located near Superior, Arizona. The soldiers surprised and killed a group of Apache warriors. Most of the Apache were killed, but from that group, 75 of them chose to leap to their death from the top of the cliff to avoid being captured by the soldiers.

The families of the Apache warriors wept when they heard the news of their tragic deaths. Legend says that the tears from their families turned to stone when they hit the ground, forming Apache tears. Many believe the stones bring good luck to those that carry them today. Science tells us a different story about the origin of the Apache tears. The small stones are actually formed when lava cools in a short time resulting in volcanic glass. I prefer the heartwarming story of Apache tears being shed during mourning.

Anyway, in Heaven there will be *no more* tears. *"The foundations of the wall of the city were adorned with all kinds of precious stones: the first foundation was jasper, the second sapphire, the third chalcedony, the fourth emerald, the fifth sardonyx, the sixth sardius, the seventh chrysolite, the eighth beryl, the ninth topaz, the tenth chrysoprase, the eleventh jacinth, and the twelfth amethyst"* (Rev. 21:18–20).

There will be *no more* tears when we take that golden walk on the street of pure gold that looks like transparent glass. It is my belief that God will give us all the desires of our hearts magnified to represent His glory, love, and magnificence. With each golden step, we will get another surprise. Alleluia!

## Will We?

Does this section in the book seem a little peculiar? Consider this: right now, we can walk through my childhood memories in *Barrio Walk*. This walk is imperfect because it is only words. Maybe the day is coming when I can take you for a walk through my barrio as it actually happens. Or perhaps, you can exchange life experiences with those who you loved on earth.

*Will we be able to go on walks with God?* Enoch, who was Noah's great-grandfather, walked with God for most of his earthly life. *"And after he became the father of Methuselah, Enoch walked with God 300 years and had other sons and daughters. Altogether, Enoch live 365 years. Enoch walked with God; then he was no more because God took him away"* (Gen. 5:21–24).

Bonus: Did you know that Methuselah lived to the age of 969 years (Gen. 6:27). There is a tree growing high in the White Mountains of Inyo County in eastern California that is nicknamed Methuselah. This old guy is a 4,852-year-old great basin bristlecone pine tree. Its confirmed age goes back to 2,831 years before Christ.

It gives me comfort when my mind takes me back for a walk on Memory Lane with my mother. During her last years of life, we talked about her favorite spiritual song called He Walks With Me. We were blessed to have mom stay with us on several extended visits to Los Angeles and Pflugerville. Irma is always singing at home and mom joined in one day. It is an incredible memory to think about Mamita's face radiating and how peaceful she looked as she got her praise on. It is one of those precious recordings etched into my heart by God – just for a moment...just to be able to play again as a reminder that she is rejoicing in His Peace.

*Will we* get to choose what our job will be in Heaven? Maybe one day be an astronaut, a scientist, an artist, a botanist, a musician, composer, teacher of any subject, an opera singer, a welcomer of those arriving in Heaven, an intercessor, a time traveler, a servant of God (Yes!), or better yet, maybe all of those at the same time.

I am thanking God in advance because one day in Heaven I might be a zoologist and gardener like Adam. I'll be able to farm the land and name the animals (Gen. 2:15). Unlike Adam, I will eat from the Tree of Life. I'm in awe of the thought of seeing this Tree of Life that yields its fruit every month (Rev. 22:2). Maybe I'll call a sloth by the name of a slow car and Cheetah will be changed to the name of my favorite car.

*Will we* hear the constant sound of a babbling brook or the continuous laughter of children? In Revelation Chapter 1, John describes the sound of God's voice being like the sound of rushing waters. The sound of heaven will be of joyous celebration and thanksgiving because it is in Heaven we will truly be in the presence of the Lord with the choir of angels. Scripture says Heaven has musical instruments. The 24 elders in Revelation 5:8 sat around the throne of God with harps. Trumpets are another instrument mentioned in Revelation 8:6. The wings of the angels sound like crashing against the shore or the sound of a mighty army according to Ezekiel 1:24. We will be able to hear sounds in Heaven that we cannot hear on Earth since all the sounds in Heaven will be full of praise for God.

*Will we* know our loved ones? The late Billy Graham[15] once said: "While the Bible doesn't answer all our questions about Heaven, I have no doubt we will recognize each other there. In fact, the Bible indicates we will know each other more fully than we do now." The Apostle Paul declared, *"Now I know in part; then I shall know fully, even as I am fully known"* (1 Cor. 13:12).

*Will we* be able to time travel? God is certainly capable of bending time and opening doors in another dimension for us. I would love to trace my ancestors all the way back to Noah's ark. It would be wonderful to witness those three young men coming out of the fiery furnace with no scent of smoke on them. God is in control of the whole universe. Perhaps we'll get to spend some time on Mars, "to get candy bars," like my son Michael would say. He also teased his older brother by saying, "Ruben went to Jupiter and came back stupidter."

*Will we* be able to be at two places at the same time? With God all things are possible. Because God is not limited by time, He may show us past events as if they were presently happening. We may be able to study history from a front-row seat. Perhaps we'll have opportunity to see the lives of our spiritual and physical ancestors lived out on earth.

*Will we* have a different sense of time? Some argue that we will not experience time in Heaven because we are told, *"The city does not need the sun or the moon to shine on it, for the glory of God gives it light, and the Lamb is its lamp"* (Rev. 21:23). If the cycle of day and night is done away with, perhaps that signals the end of time — or at least our measurement of time.

Also, we know that God exists apart from time (2 Pet. 3:8), so perhaps those dwelling with Him will also be outside of time.

*Will we* be able to experience a thousand years in a day? Consider if one day is like a thousand years with the Lord, then the average human life (70 years), would run 25 million years. Hopefully that one day is more like a Sunday rather than our Monday.

*Will we* receive crowns in Heaven? The Bible mentions five different crowns a person can receive in Heaven. The *imperishable crown* is described in 1 Corinthians 9:24–25. The *crown of righteousness* is described by the Apostle Paul in 2 Timothy 4:8. The *crown of life* is mentioned in Revelation 2:10. The *crown of rejoicing* is referenced in 1 Thessalonians 2:19. And finally, the *crown of glory* is described by Peter in 1 Peter 5:4. My prayer is to receive all five so I can I lay them at the feet of Jesus and spend more time with Him.

*Will we* meet St. Peter at the gate? No, only God can judge whether someone gets into Heaven. The common belief that St. Peter will be at the gates has been the subject of numerous jokes, including this one: *A preacher and a bus driver went to Heaven. The bus driver got an enormous, beautiful mansion with many large rooms. The preacher only received a one-room cottage, so he asked St. Peter to explain. The preacher said, "How come I only get a very small place and the bus driver got that big mansion? I've preached the Good News all my life!" St. Peter replied, "It's a matter of results. When you preached, people fell asleep. When the bus driver drove, people prayed."*

*Will we* be able to meet the characters from the Bible? I would love to talk to Jabez to find out exactly how God blessed him—*I need closure.* You can read about Jabez in 1 Chronicles 4:9–10.

*Will we* be able to speak or understand other languages? I might or might not be able to tell you until we are there.

*"What no eye has seen, nor ear heard, nor the heart of man imagined"* (1 Cor. 2:9). This gives us enormous freedom to imagine and the knowledge of other languages we will never quite understand while still here on earth. So for now I will continue practicing rolling my r's and enunciating properly.

*Will we* be able to see more colors? Yes, because our human minds are limited. How can we put into words a description of the color of Jesus's transformation? *"And he was transfigured before them, and his face shone like the sun, and his clothes became white as light"* (Matt. 17:2). What color is "shone like the sun" and "white as light"?

Will we be able to sing like and with the angels? We will sing (Rev. 15:3–4). Those who could never carry a tune on earth will be able to sing in heaven and never grow tired of giving glory to the Lamb. Irma and I once experienced the most beautiful form of worship at Times Square Church in New York City. People were singing the same song in various languages; however, it was not confusing. The melody was in complete harmony with an extra dose of Holy Spirit anointing. Oily tears leaked from our eyes that day.

Will we have a job in Heaven? Our work will be restful. *"No longer will there be anything accursed, but the throne of God and of the Lamb will be in it, and his servants will serve him"* (Rev. 22:3).

Will we have a pecking order in Heaven? Matthew 5:9 certainly seems to imply a hierarchy of some description: *"Whosoever therefore shall break one of these least commandments, and shall teach men so, he shall be called the least in the kingdom of heaven: but whosoever shall do and teach them, the same shall be called great in the kingdom of heaven."*

Can we get kicked out of Heaven? No, the amazing thing about our salvation is that we have been given a new nature. When Jesus returns or we die and go to Heaven, we will receive our new bodies. And God's very nature will be manifested through us. To put it another way, we won't have a nature that can sin or fall, like Lucifer did. The position God has given us is way above anything that Satan had because God has given us Himself! This new nature scripture says:

*"No one who is born of God practices sin, because His seed abides in him; and he cannot sin, because he is born of God"* (1 Jn. 3:9).

I've heard various testimonies from others that gives them comfort about individuals that have gone to live in Heaven. My sister Anita told me that she and her husband Danny (he died of cancer at age 38) had a conversation shortly before he died. She asked him if he would send pennies from Heaven to remind her of him. Danny said, *"I'm a big spender, I'll send you dimes."* During her recent stay with us in Texas, I found two dimes at two different spots. Is it coincidence or is it Heaven sent?

We remember our deceased loved ones in many ways. It might be the smell of oranges, a hummingbird close by, a beautiful red cardinal, a butterfly, seeing someone who resembles your loved one, a gentle breeze, a gentle touch when nothing is there, the scent of their cologne or perfume, the smell of their brand of cigarette, hearing their favorite song, a vivid dream, a shadow in the room, a picture, remembering their words — these are all encouraging signs from God that they live and we will see them again.

Pastor Hector Gonzalez once told me to remember: *"We are not human beings having a spiritual experience, we are spiritual beings having a human experience."* He also told me, *"We only have this hour, so enjoy this moment. When you offer encouragement to others, it takes away your pain."* In his last days, he demonstrated this as he was receiving dialysis. I went with him once to understand the process. I watched many patients arriving by ambulance. Pastor Gonzalez walked in with cinnamon rolls to share and announcing what a blessed man he was. It is my understanding, he later passed away at the dialysis center. I was told when he walked in, the attendant asked him how he was. He responded, "I'm blessed, I'm blessed!" He then collapsed and was welcomed into Heaven by Jesus. Pastor Hector had *no fear* at his moment of death, and neither should we.

*"Rejoice! I will say it again: Rejoice!* (Phil. 4:4).

**Golden Step #14: Have no fear, Jesus is waiting for us.**

# CHAPTER 15

## THE RIVER OF WATER OF LIFE

*"And He showed me a pure <u>river of water of life</u>, clear as crystal, proceeding from the throne of God and of the Lamb"* (Isa. 41:13).

Waterfalls have always fascinated me. I've been blessed to visit several waterfalls over the course of my life. It was incredible to see all the waterfalls coming down the Alaskan mountains as the snow melted in June. During that visit to Alaska, we were able to drink water directly from a trickling cascade near Ketchikan. We were also blessed to have our boat guide back into the glacier so a small waterfall from it fell directly into our boat.

Dunn's River Fall in Ocho Rios is beautiful as the water cascades peacefully into the Caribbean Sea. On one of our visits, we had a young Jamaican man as a tour guide. He wore a bright yellow vest that had bold, black letters "FALL INSTRUCTOR" on the backside. His job was to help tourists climb up the falls. As I watched him, he suddenly slipped and fell. He was surprised and looked somewhat embarrassed. As I helped him up, I could not resist saying, "Okay, help me understand...your vest says 'Fall Instructor' on it because you show people how to fall down?" He was annoyed and said, "Not funny, Mon!" I had a good chuckle that day, and Irma pulled me away as she told me to leave him alone.

Multnomah Falls near Portland, Oregon, offers serenity in a forest setting. The roaring sound of Niagara Falls is unbelievable. All these waterfalls show the power and magnificence of God. Niagara Falls has 757,500 gallons of water flowing over its top every second.[16] The tallest waterfall in the world is Angels Falls in Venezuela at 3,212 feet. It is higher than three Eiffel towers stacked on top of each other. But the biggest one in the world is Khone Falls located in Laos. It is more than 35,000 feet wide (166 football fields), and 2,500,000 gallons of water flow over the top every second (three times more than Niagara Falls).

All the waterfalls on earth combined will be weak in comparison to the Water of Life that is waiting for us in Heaven. We will drink from the well of salvation from that same Source, just like the Samaritan woman, and never thirst again.

## Cristo Redentor

Christ the Redeemer[17] is an Art Deco statue of Jesus Christ in Rio de Janeiro, Brazil, that was constructed between 1922 and 1931; the statue is 98 feet high plus a pedestal measuring 26 feet. The arms of this statute stretch 92 feet wide. From the top of Corcovado Mountain, you can see Copacabana Beach and the beautiful waters of the Atlantic Ocean.

Irma and I were blessed to visit the location in 2008 as part of our Christian bucket list. The setting is spectacular as the statute overlooks the city of Rio de Janeiro. On the day we went, it was cloudy, and the face of the statute was covered by clouds. It was a disappointment until we prayed and the clouds opened momentarily. It was long enough to take some photos. My eyes were full of tears of joy as our guide laid on the ground to take a picture of us. It was a precious moment God made—just for us.

As remarkable as that visit to Brazil was, it is rubbish compared to when we come face-to-face with our Lord. The Christ the Redeemer statute is just a manmade stone monument. It has eyes but cannot see, has a mouth but cannot speak, has ears but cannot hear, has hands but cannot feel, and has feet but cannot walk. Statutes cannot utter a sound in their throats. *"Those who make them will be like them and so will all who trust in them"* (Ps. 115:8).

Our Lord is our refuge and our strength, the Son of God, the Lamb of God, the Messiah, the Way, the Truth, and the Life, the Light of the World, the Prince of Peace, the Good Shepherd, the Lion of Judah, and the King of Kings. And that's just the short list. Need I say more? Meeting Jesus in Heaven will be indescribable!

Christ the Redeemer, Rio de Janeiro, Brazil.

## Is Heaven a Real Place?

Heaven is a place, just as much as Phoenix, Arizona, and Boulder, Colorado.

Everyone wants to go to Heaven, but no one wants to die. Maybe if the unbeliever were certain about Heaven like we are, they would be able to live in anticipation of getting there instead of living in skepticism. They would know there is more to life than being born, living, dying, and then being buried in the ground. I always look forward to my next visit to my hometown in Phoenix and love going back to Boulder where I attended school. Boulder is the setting where Mork and Mindy once lived, and it is fun to visit Pearl Street Mall. Phoenix has plenty of sunshine along with my brothers and sisters, nephews, and nieces, and lots of cousins. Both places are real but temporary; only Heaven (and Hell) is forever.

The most important fact is that Heaven is a real place where believers like us will spend eternity. Read the words Jesus said on the night before he was crucified:

*Do not let your hearts be troubled. Trust in God; trust also in me. In my _Father's house_ are many rooms; if it were not so, I would have told you. I am going there to prepare a _place_ for you. And if I go and prepare a _place_ for you, I will come back and take you to be with me that you also may be where I am* (Jn. 14:1–3).

Twice in these three verses Jesus calls Heaven a place. Jesus also tells us in these verses that Heaven ("my Father's house") is a real place. Just as real as Phoenix and Boulder, just as real as wherever you call home now. Heaven is a real place filled with real people, which is why the Bible sometimes compares heaven to a house with many rooms, and it also referred to it as the Holy City, the new Jerusalem, a dwelling of God with His people (Rev. 21). God also promises, *"To him who is thirsty, I will give to drink without cost from* *the <u>spring of the water of Life</u>. He who overcomes will inherit all this, and I will be his God and he will be my son"* (Rev. 21: 6–7).

A few days ago, I had the privilege of talking to one of dad's first cousins, Barbara Gonzales Hernandez, who is in her mid-nineties. I call her my tia out of respect and I always enjoy talking with her. She told me about the early days in Phoenix during the Great Depression (1929–1941) and the poverty they experienced during those years. She said her dad, my great-uncle Pedro, had to dig a well as there was no running water. She described how this well became dry and they had to borrow water from the Quihuiz family, who lived close by in the Phoenix Sonorita barrio. Times were tough for them because there was no electricity. She chuckled when she told me their house was so dark at night that they bumped into each other. I cannot imagine living in Phoenix without air-conditioning or a swamp cooler. I'm thankful Heaven has plenty of light and water to drink *without* cost.

Heaven is where God has established His Kingdom. His throne is there, the angels are there, and the Lord Jesus Christ is in Heaven. We will be citizens of Heaven. Philippians 3:20 tells us plainly *"that our citizenship is in heaven. And we eagerly await a Savior from there, the Lord Jesus Christ."*

**Side note**: During her editing of my writing, Irma told me she had a clearer picture in her mind as she read about Heaven. She told me it created an image that what she was seeing was like a ball being bounced inside a pinball machine. She envisioned many colors of pixeled lights shining like stars and rainbows. This was combined with a swift but gentle flow of wind and the sound of a babbling brook. Her trance included a sweet smell in the air that had various scents: cinnamon bread being baked, flowers from a magnolia tree, rain, coffee, vanilla, and freshly cut grass.

All these scents were somehow combined, but each one was also distinct.

She told me her inner soul was filled with excitement as she was imagining the throne, the angels, and our Lord Jesus Christ. As she described all of this, her eyes twinkled with joy as she exclaimed, "This is what Heaven will be like and soon will be my reality!" (I wish I would have recorded how she looked when she told me about it.)

This is an anticipation that can be felt by those of us who anxiously wait for our entrance into our Forever Home. Earth is not our home; we are just passing through doing what we can to invite others on our *Golden Walk*. True believers do not leave church in a building. They carry it with them, along with others, all the way into Heaven.

Once we die, we will be there immediately. We can be sure of that by reading what Jesus told the thief on the Cross, *"Today you will be with me in paradise"* (Lk. 23:43). Since those words, somewhere in paradise today is that same thief strutting like a *vato* on his Golden Walk in Heaven.

## How Far Away Is Heaven?

The Bible gives us a hint that heaven is not as far away as we might think. As humans we sometimes think it must be outside our present universe. That's why there is the Spanish Christian song called *"Más allá del sol"* where lyrics tell of Heaven being further than the sun. The sun is about 93 million miles away from us. If we could drive a car there at 65 miles per hour non-stop, it would take about 163 years to drive there. However, it's a common belief that we will be present with Christ when we are absent from our body when we die. How then, can that be possible if Heaven is beyond the Milky Way galaxy? How will we be there in an instant when it is further than the sun? *Because with God, all things are possible!*

Hebrews 12:22–24 tells us something amazing about how Jesus has brought Heaven to us: *"But You have come to Mount Zion, to the heavenly Jerusalem, the city of the living God. You have come to thousands upon thousands of angels in joyful assembly, to the church of the firstborn, whose names are written in heaven. You have come to God, the judge of all men, to the spirits of righteous men made perfect, to Jesus the mediator of a new covenant, and to the sprinkled blood that speaks a better word than the blood of Abel."*

My goldmine, my *New Geneva Study Bible,* helped me to understand the scripture above.

It tells me Jesus' presence in the heaven (Mt. Zion) explains its atmosphere of joy and confidence. The blood of Abel cried for vengeance from the ground in Genesis 4:10. The blood of Jesus, compared to Abel's, speaks better words, that is, His blood cries out for the forgiveness for the children of God.

The writer is comparing Mt. Sinai (old covenant/before Christ) with Mt. Zion (new covenant/after Jesus). Under the old covenant no one could come near God except under very strict conditions. That's why the mountain shook with thunder and lightning. Take notice of the three times the words "you have come" are underlined. The writer of Hebrews uses the Greek word "eggizo," which means "to come near" or "to approach closely." But now in Christ we have been brought near to Heavenly realities. In other words, the writer is saying:

We're not that far from heaven because Jesus made a Way. We're not that far from the angels because of Christ.

We're not that far from our loved ones in heaven because Jesus prepared a place for them.

We're not that far from God because Jesus is there sitting next to Him on His Right Side.

We're not that far from Jesus himself because He shed His Blood for the remission of our sins.

Heaven is a real place, it's where Jesus is right now, and it's not far away from us.

Rejoice! The Kingdom of God is not that far from us.

## Seven Scriptures about Heaven

- ❖ **A city designed and built by God (Heb. 11:10).** God is the architect and builder of Heaven. It is perfect with its twelve gates and twelve angels at the gates. Each gate has the names of the twelve tribes of the children of Israel written on them.

- ❖ **Where God is and watches over us. (Ps. 33:13).** The Lord looks from Heaven; He sees all the sons of men. God cares about each one of us so much that he even knows how many hairs we have on our head. It makes my head itchy and I scratch it when I think about the average hair count on a human head. Everyone has about 100,000 hairs and God can count each one of them. There are approximately 7,660,000,000 people on earth. That means God knows the current and changing status of 7,660,000,000,000,000 hairs on human heads. Scratch, scratch—there goes another hair.

- ❖ **The Father's house (Jn. 14:2).** When you think about your childhood home, it comes with the privilege of helping yourself with what's in the refrigerator. I wonder if there will be a picture of us on the refrigerator in Heaven.

❖ **Where Christ is today (Acts 1:11).**When Jesus ascended into Heaven, two men dressed in white apparel stood by the disciples and said, *"Men of Galilee, why do you stand gazing up into Heaven? This same Jesus, who was taken up from you into Heaven will so come in like manner as you saw Him go into Heaven."* The return of Christ to earth will be wonderful.

❖ **Where Christians go when they die (Phil. 1:21–23).** Here it is clearly, *"For to me, to live is Christ, and to die is gain. If I am to go on living in my body, this will mean fruitful labor for me. Yet what shall I choose? I do not know! I am torn between the two: I desire to depart and be with Christ..."* We want to be in Heaven with Jesus but we don't want to leave our loved ones on earth. If I had to choose right now...Hasta la vista, goodbye my peeps! I'll see you there.

❖ **Paradise (Lk. 23:43).** This reference is from the scene at the crucifixion when Jesus pardons the penitent thief. I have made it a point to say they *rejoice in paradise* rather than they rest in peace. Can you imagine the kindness in our Lord's eyes when He forgave the thief?

❖ **A better country (Hebrews 11:15-16).** We will be satisfied when we find our better country, one that God has prepared for us. After visiting Spain, I tried to convince Irma that's where we needed to live. Didn't work — I'm still Home Sweet Home in Pflugerville, Texas.

Anyone who has studied the book of Revelation has read that Heaven is a place where the great street of the city is paved with gold, the gates are made of a single pearl, and the walls made of precious jewels.

Most images about Heaven come from Revelation 21. This chapter offers us the most extended picture of Heaven in the entire Bible. If you ask me if I believe those things are literally true, the answer is yes and no. Yes, they are literally true but no, Heaven won't be anything like we imagine. It will be much greater. My belief is as we journey in Heaven, we will experience endless new sensations felt by our five senses. Yes, we will see twelve gates, each made from a single pearl. The great street of Heaven is made of pure gold, like transparent glass.

Here's a humorous story that references the street made of gold:

This ancient story is of a rich man who, on his death bed, negotiated with God to allow him to bring his earthly treasures with him when he arrived in Heaven. God's reaction was that this was a most unusual request. But since this man had been exceptionally faithful, permission was granted to bring along just one suitcase.

The time arrived, and the man presented himself at the pearly gates with suitcase in hand carried with both hands because of the weight. It was because the rich man had stuffed it with as many bars of gold bullion as would fit. St. Peter said, "Sorry, you know the rules — you can't take it with you." But the man protested, "God said I could ... one suitcase." St. Peter checked, found out that this one would be an exception, prepared to let the man enter, but then said,

"OK, but I will have to examine the contents before you pass."
He took the suitcase, opened it, saw the gold bars, and asked
quizzically, "Why did You bring *pavement*?"

John wrote about a street paved with gold, and I do not
doubt his words. He simply wrote what he saw in his vision
of Heaven. John's words are literally true. The above joke
also serves to tell us that the things we value so highly in this
life will be used to pave the street in Heaven.

## Drinking from the Well of Salvation

What was the significance of the woman at the well, and
why is her tale important to Christian believers?

In John 4:1–42 there is a lengthy conversation between
Jesus and a Samaritan woman. She is never named, yet her
encounter with Jesus is the longest between the Messiah and
any other individual in the Gospel of John. Note: Please read
this story in your Bible.

This takes place when Jesus traveling through Samaria on
the way to Galilee sat down at a well in the town of Sychar.
It was about noon, and while His disciples were in town
buying food, Jesus encountered a Samaritan woman coming
to draw water from the well. He asked her for a drink, and
their talk took off from there—concluding in her salvation
and many more from her town.

The woman was surprised He was talking to her as Jews
had no dealings with Samaritans (verse 9). The Jews and
Samaritans felt contempt for each other. It should be noted
that in those days many Jews would take the long road when
going between Galilee and Judea just to avoid Samaria. They
even crossed the Jordan River twice rather than stepping foot
in Samaria.

It should be noted that sometimes we as Christians avoid those considered undesirable. Perhaps it is easier to welcome someone who is like us or we tend pay more attention to those individuals who may have more to offer because of their position or financial status. The Samaritan woman was representing the lowest of the low — a female in a society where women were demeaned and disregarded. She represents us as sinners prior to accepting Christ, before we drank from His Living Water.

In verse 10 Jesus offers the gift of God — salvation. Our Lord still offers this free gift to us now. He loves *everyone* the same and does not want *anyone* to perish but for *all* to have eternal life. *"For the wages of sin is death, but the gift of God is eternal life in Christ Jesus our Lord"* (Rom. 6:23).

The woman pointed out that Jesus had no cup and then asked about this so-called living water as well as asking if He was greater than Jacob. While the story does not tell whether her tone was sarcastic, rhetorical, or fully sincere, maybe she was just being facetious (verses 11–12). Sometimes when the plan of salvation is heard by the non-believer, it does not make sense. It may also present a threat because we don't want to change our current way of life. Some people don't think it is cool to be Christian. I think it is as cool as you can get; so much that my self-proclaimed nickname is *Frosty*. I also call some of those closest to me by that name.

In verse 13 Jesus provides a clear, earnest answer while elaborating on this living water. When she heard the explanation, she reacted. *"Faith comes from hearing and hearing by the word of God"* (Rom. 10:17). Keep planting seeds of salvation to those around — the rewards are eternal.

It prompted her to ask Him for this water (verse 15).

That's when Jesus shifted to the next phase of their dialogue, which reveals that not only did He have what she needed, but He knew things about her that caught her completely off guard — that she had been married five times and was not married to her current man (v. 18). She was probably having a rough time in life as she had five previous husbands and was living with a man that had not become her 6th husband. Life for me was beyond difficult and I probably would not be here today without my repentance and new life in Christ.

She then referred to Jesus as a prophet and began to speak on religious matters, specifically noting that Jews believe the place they must worship is Jerusalem (v. 20).

"Woman," Jesus replied, "believe me, a time is coming when you will worship the Father neither on this mountain nor in Jerusalem. You Samaritans worship what you do not know; we worship what we do know, for salvation is from the Jews. Yet a time is coming and has now come when the true worshipers will worship the Father in the Spirit and in truth, for they are the kind of worshipers the Father seeks. God is spirit, and his worshipers must worship in the Spirit and in truth" (v. 21–24).

The story of the woman at the well is a rich example of love, truth, redemption, and acceptance. The best part about it, not only does Jesus accept her, but He still accepts us too. It is dependent on our faith and believing He is the Messiah. He said it plainly when the Samaritan woman spoke about the coming Messiah. Their conversation ended when he told her: *"I who speak to you, am He"* (Jn. 4:26).

She was blessed to have had a holy encounter with Christ because she received eternal salvation. And her testimony convinces an entire town to believe too.

Is it time for you to drink from the well of salvation? *Sometimes you must hit rock bottom to find the Rock at the bottom!*

## My Attempt to Write a Song about the Well of Salvation:

"The Well of Salvation"
I knew my life was wrong and my destiny was hell
Until I took a drink of You from that salvation well
My thirst was not quenched after 30 years of drinking
Only You could change my heart to stop this soul from sinking
Chorus:
*Lord, Drench me in Your Living Tide*
*Calm the storms that brew inside*
*Cover me with Your miraculous rain*
*Washing my soul clean of every stain*
No more thirsty days because You've done Your part
Let your living water nourish the root system of my heart.
The Joy of the Lord is my strength, in you I put my trust
Storing my treasures in Heaven, where they cannot rust
Chorus
*Lord, Drench me in Your Living Tide*
*Calm the storms that brew inside*
*Drown me with Your Peace and Love*
*Pour down some Goodness from above*
Soaked in Living Water to expand the way I think
Watching upwards for what will happen in a blink
Thank you for Your Living Water from the salvation well
My destiny is Heaven, you drowned the fires of hell.
Chorus
*As long as You lead the Way*
*To the salvation well today*
*Never will I thirst again*
*Through you my battle has been won*

*"And the Spirit and the bride say, "Come!" And let him who hears say, "Come!" And let him who thirsts come. Whoever desires, let him take the water of life freely"* (Rev. 22:17).

**Golden Step #15: Drink from His Living Water and never thirst again.**

# CHAPTER 16

## LIKE THE ROAR OF A LION

*"And He gave a loud shout <u>like the roar of a lion</u>. When He shouted, the voices of seven thunders spoke."* (Rev. 10:3).

There are seven times in the book of Revelations when the Lord says, "To him who overcomes I will give." He is encouraging us to overcome the trials of life by walking steady. We will have to enter Heaven through the narrow gate by walking with a narrow gait. Narrow gait? This is a person's manner of walking. A narrow gait describes the "straight and narrow" path to Heaven.

Did you know the term "straight and narrow" comes from the Bible in Matthew 7:14: *Broad is the way that is the path of destruction but* narrow *is the gate and* straight *is the way which leads to the House of God, and only a few find it."* There is an eternity of blessings and surprises waiting for us by following wisdom into Heaven. Golden Walk is about walking our earthly life so we finish victoriously when we enter into the presence of God.

## Blessings and Surprises

When we arrive in Heaven, it will be full of continuous surprises. On a recent road trip, my wife and I seemed to have our face stuck in "drop jaw" syndrome. We were blessed to spend four nights in Eureka Springs, Arkansas. The winding roads full of lush forest was gluttony to the eyes of a dude from Phoenix. The peaceful nights in the calm of a cabin that seemed to be wrapped in a blanket of pine trees is beyond description. My morning walks refreshed my soul as I was full of wonder with every step. The scent of the fresh rain was an excellent appetizer for the anticipation of the day. The lake below us looked like a large skating rink I could walk on. Hmmm? Here's a thought about walking on water:

Peter was able to walk on water when he got out of the boat to go to Jesus. Much of the focus of this story is about Peter sinking into the water because he took his eyes off Jesus. Peter became afraid when he saw the waves and started to sink before he reached our Lord. We miss a great point in this story if we only consider Peter's failure. Have you ever wondered how Peter got back into the boat? The answer is Jesus took a hold of Him, and Peter was able to walk back into the boat just like he had when he walked on water. Just because we failed once doesn't mean our walk is over. Let the Lord take hold of your hand and continue walking with Him all the way to Heaven.

God directed my path to meet so many wonderful people during our stay in the Ozark Mountains. During the Holy Land Tour, I met author Charles Robinson at the lesson of the Tabernacle. I spoke to Brother Robinson briefly after Pastor Joel Perales purchased his book, *Punching the Sun*, for me (Pastor insisted on gifting it to me). When I told Brother Rob I was almost finished with my third Christian book, he advised me to roar like a lion when sharing my faith. He continued by telling me how the ground shakes when a lion roars. He instructed me to be bold like a lion when sharing the good news. In his book *Punching the Sun*, it says, "Now is the time to awaken from our sleep and roar, not only roar but run, run fast the life set before us."[18] So, with my remaining days, I promise to roar about my faith and run to tell others rather than walk. Currently, Charles Robinson and his wife, Eloisa, serve at the Great Passion Play in Eureka Springs. They are missionaries; you can learn more about them at www.servantsofthesavior.net. It was a pleasure meeting you. Below is the *afterword* from *Punching the Sun*.

To him that overcometh will I give to eat at the tree of life, which is in the midst of the paradise of God. He that overcometh shall not be hurt of the second death. To him that overcometh will I give to eat of the hidden manna, and will give him a white stone, and in the stone a new name written, which no man knoweth saving he that receiveth it. And he that overcometh, and keepeth my works unto the end, to him will I give power over the nations: And he shall rule them with a rod of iron; as vessels of a potter shall be broke to shivers, even as I received of my Father. And I will give him the morning star. He that overcometh, the same shall be clothed in white raiment; and I will not blot out his name out of the book of life, but I will confess his name before my Father and before His angels. Him that overcometh will I make a pillar in the temple of my God, and he shall go no more out; and I will write upon him the name of my God, and the name of the city of God, which is the new Jerusalem, which cometh down out of heaven from my God: and I will write upon him my new name. To him that overcometh will I grant to sit with me in my throne, even as I also overcame, and am set down with my Father in his throne.

(Revelation 2:7, 11, 17, 26–28, 3:5, 12, 21)

Later that day, I had the pleasure of meeting an artist named Jack E. Dawson at the Sacred Arts Museum and art gallery. I was overwhelmed by the 33 paintings on display from Mr. Dawson's collection. Each painting has hidden messages and tells a story. His wife, Nancy, enthusiastically talked about the paintings as she showed groups the secreted meanings in the paintings. You will be blessed if you visit his website at www.BitterSweetGallery.com. Irma and I were mesmerized by the talent and the secret codes displayed on each painting.

I purchased an 11 × 14 print framed called "Reviewing the Troops." Please look for this painting on the website. It is a painting of President George Washington saluting the troops of past and present wars in front of the Vietnam Wall. This painting has a small bronze plate with a scripture from Philippians 2:29 underneath it. *"Welcome him in the Lord with great joy and honor men like him."*

Brother Dawson had a countenance full of tranquility, peace, and humility. This saintlike artist was kind enough to sign the print and thanked me for my service in Vietnam. When I shook hands with him, my memory kicked in, and I was able to tell him, "I am more honored shaking hands with you more than the time when I shook hands with Willie Mays." He seemed to blush and told me he had not received a compliment like that one. His work is anointed, and I know Jack's work has led many to follow Christ. Perhaps there is a message waiting *just for you* in one of his paintings.

The world-renowned Great Passion Play and Christ of the Ozarks alone are enough reason to visit this area. At the Passion Play the night was chilly but blankets were provided, and there was lots of popcorn. The time at this 4,000-seat outdoor amphitheater is a memory I will never forget. My hope is to organize at least one tour to take others with us in the upcoming years. I don't want to give you all the details now, or else I'll have to charge you the full price of admission.

At one point in our four-day vacay, God matched us up in the parking lot with the chef from a restaurant where we had just eaten. He was a new believer named Joseph, and I blessed him with a copy of *Barrio Walk*. It is my prayer he receives the encouragement from this book to help him stay on God's purpose for his life. He gave us many insider tips on where to eat and what to see. One of his recommendations was for a fishing guide/barber from Tall Tales Barbershop.

Pastor Joel Perales and I had a memorable time on the White River on his birthday. We went out with our fishing guide but did not get haircuts. What we received was seven large rainbow trout and much relaxation near the Beaver Dam. Pastor was able to land four fish before I caught my first one. He teased me and offered me the Biblical advice to "cast my net on the other side." When I did, poof, I brought in a perfect 20-inch rainbow trout. We laughed as God continued to surprise us. We caught three fish that were over 16 inches and had to release one as the limit allowed for two. While fishing, I sang happy birthday to Pastor with every fish he caught as he outfished me five to two.

Our guide serenaded him with the birthday song in the voice of Edith Bunker. It probably scared several fish away but made a great memory. Later that evening back at the cabin, we grilled the trout with lots of lemon. The bigger trout tasted like salmon. The celebration continued with a cake made by Irma with melted chocolate frosting and topped with an abundance of pecans. The evening was full of praise — what a blessing.

Heaven will be full of unexpected *blessings and surprises* for eternity. In Denver, we received many more simple pleasures — days full of memories, visiting with old friends, meeting new friends, making friends with some we may never see again. Until that one day — when we are all Home with our Heavenly Father. It was good for my heart to see "Cool Breeze" and his wife, Janet. Thank you, Al, for the fabulous home-cooked meal; each bite was incredible.

We had the pleasure of spending time with Julian Cordova and his family. His kindness was genuine, and his friendship is a treasure. Hearing him praise at his home on his piano was spectacular. He has a special sense of dry humor to go with his serious facade. May God continue to bless them and their chain of Chubby's restaurants that have served Denver residents for years.

Going back to Boulder was special; I had the privilege of serving as postmaster there in 1995. We visited Boulder Canyon to see the rushing stream speeding through the mountains. There were many students from my alma mater (University of Colorado) floating down this river on inner tubes. The area is a prelude to what Heaven will look like on a minor scale. It was full of light and life and had so many opportunities to take pictures. If only we could stretch or stall time at places that leave you with your mouth wide open in awe. Guess what? Those days are just ahead of us when we finish our walk on earth.

God continued to have us meet people on our journey home. At the Garden of the Gods, we met two young ladies (from Phoenix and Dallas). They were full of joy and laughter as they told us to visit Manitou Springs. They advised us to take a cup to drink from the crystal clear spring water. We followed their advice and were blessed to see this charming town with refreshing water running next to it. This town was founded for its natural mineral springs. The main road through the center of town was one of the direct paths to the base of Pike's Peak. It is interesting to us how God kept drawing us to water. After all the Bible does say, *"But whoever drinks the water I give them will never thirst. Indeed, the water I give them will become in them a spring of water welling up to eternal life"* (Jn. 4:14).

We met a couple in Manitou Springs that took our picture next to an old train near the downtown area. It was close to the springs, and the sound of the water added to the ambiance. This couple was from Dripping Springs, Texas, and were accompanied by their granddaughter named Lily. This couple told us to stop by Palo Duro Canyon. It is a beautiful gem near Amarillo, Texas. This is a must-stop if you are passing near Amarillo. We had no intention of stopping at either Manitou Springs or Palo Duro Canyon. Heaven will be like these two unplanned stops because we will not know what to expect at the next blessing God has in store for us.

Palo Duro is the second-largest canyon in the United States. It is roughly 120 miles long and has an average width of 6 miles. There are spots where the canyon reaches a width of 20 miles. Its depth is around 820 feet, but in some locations it increases to 1,000 feet. Palo Duro Canyon has been named the "Grand Canyon of Texas" both for its size and for its dramatic geological features. It has multicolored layers of rock and steep mesa walls that are like those of its cousin — the Grand Canyon. Palo Duro was formed by the Prairie Dog Town Fork Red River.

At the first lookout point, we met a couple with their daughter, who told us they were on their way to the Grand Canyon. He was excited about hiking to a formation in Palo Duro called the Lighthouse. It is a three-plus-mile hike to the Lighthouse, and I told my new friend I would wave to him from the top of the canyon. It was already nearly 90 degrees before noon.

*We as believers need to be like a lighthouse that shines in the darkness to lead others into the safe harbor of Heaven. We need to shine like Jesus so others can clearly see the Way, the Truth, and the Life.*

During our time away from home I gave away business cards and several copies of *Barrio Walk* and *Broken Walk* to various individuals. My aim is to have the scriptures in these books *roar like a lion* about Jesus. The books will allow readers see scriptures that I did not know about until age 47. May the words in these two books along with *Golden Walk* flow like living water to nourish the root system of each heart and soul of the person who reads them.

Irma and I took a walk to the gift shop at Palo Duro. The mature woman working from behind the circular glassed display was immediately drawn to me. She looked at me and said, "You look so familiar — do I know you from some-where?" I answered with a firm roar by saying, "It's because I am your brother in Christ!" She looked flabbergasted and mumbled, "I'm not so sure about that!" At this point, Irma opened the window of witnessing opportunity by saying, "My husband is an author and has written two books." Nice assist, Sweetie!

This allowed me to tell her about *Broken Walk*, and she was immediately moved to tears as I told her about my problems with alcohol. She told me she had an alcoholic brother who was unable to conquer this addiction. Meanwhile, customers were making purchases, and I reassured her I would not leave until we finished our conversation. As I was waiting, I selected a Palo Duro ballcap for myself and proceeded to the other side of the glass enclosure to pay. I was able to finish my conversation with the woman behind the counter by telling her about numbering our days. *"Teach us to number our days, that we may gain a heart of wisdom"* (Ps. 90:12). I mentioned that His Word is like a vision for each of us. It gives us direction so we, like sleeping lions, can wake up from our slumber and roar. I continued by telling her to let her brother know he cannot beat alcoholism without Jesus. She promised me she would purchase the book and read it prior to giving it to her brother. (I believe the book will benefit her as much as her sibling.) She was in tears by this point. I explained that numbering our days begins with *one,* as *that's all we have.* If we take care of *today* continuously, we are then able to roar and run fast the race of life He has set before us! Glory to God — thank you for allowing me to speak these words.

Even though there were several individuals in the gift shop, it was like we were the only two persons there. God provided this moment — just for us. From the corner of my eye, I saw the man enter who was about to go hiking with his family to the Lighthouse. I asked Irma to hand me another hat like mine. It was to provide my new hatless friend with covering as he hiked. The saleswoman was surprised by this gesture and now was in tears; she said, "Blessings! Blessings!" as we departed.

When I gave my new friend his hat, he reacted like he had just won the lottery. His young daughter remarked, "I can't believe someone you just met bought you a hat for no reason." We left the gift shop quickly and quietly knowing we left an impression for the Glory of God alone. *Preaching about Jesus does not solely come from behind the pulpit.* Thank you, Lord, for blessing us so we can be a blessing.

My next surprise of the trip came when I discovered a tick attached the back of my leg at a Winters, Texas, comfort stop. It ticked me off to see what I thought was a skin tag move its reddish, small legs in the bright sunlight. When I saw the legs move, it really *ticked* me off. Then I chuckled and said, "Who says you can't show an old dog (me) new ticks?" LOL. Irma carefully removed it, and we applied 99.9% hand disinfectant (there's an abundance because of COVID -19) to the small wound. It was like God pruning another remora of sin to help me abide in Him and bear fruit. It could also represent a person who hears the Word but then becomes detached from Jesus. *Apart from Him, we can do nothing!* "For what hope have the godless when they are cut off, when God takes away their life?" (Job 27:8).

As I prayed not to get Lyme disease, good news came in a phone call as we neared our home. My daughter-in-law, Misti, could barely contain herself as she told us about my upcoming birthday gift in August. She knows how much I like art, so guess who has VIP admission to the van Gogh exhibit in Dallas Texas? Thank you so much!

When we arrived at our home in Pflugerville after two weeks, there was a box sitting on our front porch. It contained a bird feeder that is squirrel-proof. Finally, I will love seeing the birds eating while "Cozy" the squirrel looks at them with pickle-colored eyes. Thank you, my sister Anita; now the birds can enjoy what once was squirrel food.

God provides many blessings and surprises along the walk of life. This is a preview to what we will receive in Heaven but magnified by our comprehension. Jesus came to give us life abundantly. We must share it with others. Start by saying the words:

I can see change coming! I am excited about the change and new friends I will encounter in the upcoming days. I am ready to share the blessings and surprises that God will give us *today*! I will never go back being the old me. With God I am going to be unafraid to be me so I can share Him without any reservation to bless others.

We are fortunate to live in the United States—and have accumulated the wealth of life experience, travel, and information in our lives thus far. We may not feel wealthy by monetary measures, but with God we are abundantly wealthy. Wealth is not just about money; it is about investing in valuable things just from living. We can become wealthier by sharing what we have gained along the way to increase our wealth together. The great things from God will always include others. God is not interested in us becoming a selfish, self-centered saint with no interest in the welfare of others. He wants us to do something that will last longer than ourselves. God blesses us so we can be a blessing to others—all the way to the next generation. (This is part of being the Fre-Generation.) Share your faith, wake up, and roar when you glorify God through your words and manner of walking. We must give hope to those who have given up on hope. This action will prosper all of us until we meet in the Kingdom of God.

**Golden Step #16: Roar like a lion about your faith...Roar so loud that the ground shakes.**

# CHAPTER 17

## THE WALLS OF JERICHO FELL

*"By faith, the walls of Jericho Fell after the army had marched round them for seven days"* (Heb. 11:30).

W hile the Israelites camped at Gilgal, Joshua went out to see the city of Jericho. As he looked at the great stone wall that surrounded the city, he must have wondered how his army could ever force its way inside. Since the people of Jericho were expecting the Israelites to attack, they had already stored sufficient provisions. When they locked the gate, they felt their city was completely secure. No one from the inside was allowed to leave Jericho while the Israelites were waiting outside ready to attack.

As Joshua walked about and wondered what to do, he saw a strange man who was dressed like a soldier and who carried a bright sword. Joshua asked, "Are you for us or for the people of Jericho?"

The stranger answered, "I am the captain of the army of the Lord."

Joshua fell on his face and worshipped. Then he asked, "What does the Lord want me to do?"

"Take off your shoes," the captain said, "for the place where you stand is holy ground."

*And the Lord let Joshua know how the Israelites were to attack.*

The Israelites were about to enter the Promised Land, but first — by faith — the walls of Jericho fell. Read this wonderful story of faith found in Joshua 5:13–6:27.

We, like the Israelites, are waiting to enter the Promised Land. To get there we must get past an entrance gate that has an enormous wall surrounding it. *"Now the wall of the city had twelve foundations, and on them were the names of the twelve apostles of the Lamb. And he who talked with me had a gold reed to measure the city, its gates, and its wall....Then he measured its wall: one hundred and forty-four cubits, according to the measure of a man, that is, of an angel"* (Rev. 21:16–17). How thick is 144 cubits?[19] The wall of Heaven is 72 feet thick. Wow! That is only one yard less than ¾ of a football field. The security of Heaven does not stop there. There are 4 walls with twelve gates and guarded by twelve angels, one at each of the gates.

The walls of the city, its length, breadth, and height are 12,000 furlongs, or 1,400 miles. Heaven is a perfect cube, the same shape as the Most Holy Place in the Tabernacle and the Temple. Try to imagine 4 walls that form a square with each side measuring 1400 miles. It's easier for me to think about it as one of the sides going from Phoenix, Arizona, to the Saint Louis Arch and another wall stretching from Mexico to Canada. Now, tilt your head back and think about 72-feet-thick walls going upward for 1400 miles. It makes my neck and brain hurt.

**Bonus note:** Siri told me: A six-foot man (like me) standing and looking out to the horizon can see approximately 5 kilometers away, (about 3 miles) as the earth's surface curves out of sight. But our ability to see extends well beyond the horizon. It depends on the amount of dust and pollution in the air, which normally limits normal vision to less than 12 miles.

All these miles of walls and then everything shines with the glory of God, like a precious jewel (Rev. 21:11). The light from the walls full of precious stones will penetrate our eyes to feed our soul with an instant form of immense joy.

The whole city of Heaven is architecturally perfect and has become the most intimate dwelling place of God.

In our human minds we think, "Really? How will we ever get past these walls?" Then we try to get in by being more good than bad. We think, "I guess the way to penetrate those walls is with accumulated good deeds while here on Earth." Wrong! There is only One Way — you'll find it in John 14:6 *"Jesus answered, I am the Way and the Truth and the Life. No one comes to the Father except through Me."* The answer for us, just like it was for the Israelites, comes from obedience by faith. When we get there, you will notice the sun and the moon are no longer needed for light as the glory of God brightens everything. We will get to see thousands and thousands of angels worshipping God. Perhaps we'll get to meet our guardian angel like the one who helped Peter in Acts 12:8. I need to get out of this earthly prison so I can experience the true freedom of pure worship. *By faith in Jesus, we will get into Heaven, it is far more beautiful than anything you will hear, see, smell, touch, think about, or feel on earth. All praise and honor to the Lamb of God!*

## Teachings from Jericho

### Lesson #1: God is in control.

The people of Israel had just crossed over the Jordan River into the land of Canaan. God miraculously stopped the water from flowing so the whole nation of Israel crossed on dry ground. *"The priests who carried the ark of the covenant of the*

*Lord stopped in the middle of the Jordan and stood on dry ground, while all Israel passed by until the whole nation had completed the crossing on dry ground"* (Josh. 3:17). They had finally arrived at the land of milk and honey God had promised to Abraham over 500 years earlier in Deuteronomy 6:3. This came after spending forty difficult years wandering in the desert of Sinai. Their first challenge in capturing the Promised Land was to overtake Jericho. However, the city of Jericho looked like an unconquerable, walled city — *But God had another plan.*

The foundation leading to the walls of Jericho was about 46 feet above ground level outside the first retaining wall.

To put this into perspective, envision a massive surrounding of protection around a small city as tall as a four-story-tall building. This was the height of the walls of Jericho. Excavations of the walls surrounding Jericho have shown two stone walls, the outer wall one was 12–15 feet high and the second one was 20–26 feet tall. After these two walls there was a smooth stone slope that angled upward at 35 degrees for an additional 35 feet. At this point, the fortification joined massive stone walls that towered even higher.

The illusion created by the two walls on the bottom and the large wall at the crest of the embankment seemed to stand nearly 10 stories in height from ground level! From this height, I'm sure the citizens of Jericho felt secure as they looked down on the army of Israel marching around silently for seven days.

It appeared to be virtually impossible to penetrate, *but not for God.* On the seventh day when the trumpets sounded, the massive walls collapsed! Alleluia!

**Lesson #2: Be obedient, keep walking in silence, and trust in God.**

During those times, research shows such cities were either taken by assault or surrounded to make the people within the walls starve into submission. Sometimes attackers would use fire or dig tunnels to weaken the stone walls. Another approach was to heap up a lot of dirt to use as a ramp. Preparation for each of these methods of assault took weeks or months. This made the invaders vulnerable to arrows or other projectiles. The plan to take over Jericho was unique in two ways.

First, the tactic was laid out by God Himself, and second, the strategy seemed to make no sense. God simply told Joshua to have the people to march *silently* around Jericho for six days, and then, after seven trips on the seventh day, to shout. You could imagine how much the people of Jericho harassed the Israel army after five or six days of marching around the wall in silence.

There is an immense difference between God's way of thinking and ours. *"For My ways are not your thoughts, nor your ways My ways"* (Isa. 55:8). The scripture in Proverbs 3 tells us we must not lean on our own understanding so He can make our path straight.

**Lesson #3: Exercise obedience, even when God's commands are hard to understand.**

Even though it seemed foolish, Joshua followed God's instructions to the letter. When the people did finally shout, the massive walls collapsed instantly, and Israel won an easy victory. It was when the people of God, by faith, followed the commands of God that the walls of Jericho fell down. On the seventh day, *"When the trumpets sounded, the army shouted,... the walls collapsed; so everyone charged straight in, and they took the city"* (Josh. 6:20).

We must never question God's purpose or instructions. We must have faith that God is who He says He is and will do what He says He will do. *"Let us hold unswervingly to the hope we profess for He who promised is faithful"* (Heb. 10:23). Here are a couple of examples when the instructions seem illogical but the result was favorable because of faith. Why did Jesus have Peter catch a fish to take a four-drachma coin to pay for their taxes? (Matt. 17:27) Why did Naaman have to dip himself seven times in the Jordan to be cured of leprosy? (2 Ki. 5:14) The answer is simple: Obedience. Good things happen when we obey God completely, especially when the situation seems impossible.

Rejoice when you receive a blessing from God such as miraculous healing. Tell others about it for the Glory of God alone. Accept salvation with no doubt of where you will spend eternity. Some people need to stop trying to earn their way into Heaven because Jesus has already knocked the wall down.

**Lesson #4: The power of God is supernatural and beyond our comprehension.**

The walls of Jericho fell instantly and completely only by the sheer power of God. As massive as they were, they collapsed just like God had promised.

God also reveals His omnipotence in Job Chapter 38 with some profound questions:

- *Where were you when I laid the foundations of the earth?* (Verse 4)

- *Where is the way to the dwelling of light? And darkness, where is its place?* (Verse 18)

- *Has the rain a father?* (Verse 28)

- *Who has put wisdom in the mind? Or who has given understanding to the heart?* (Verse 36)

Only God can make a heart start beating. Only God can change a stone heart filled with anger and selfishness into one full of the love of Jesus. Only God exhales His breath of life into a newborn baby as the infant takes its first breath. Only God inhales (takes back) His breath of life when we take our last breath.

**Lesson #5: We must demonstrate an uncompromising faith to God.**

*"By faith, the walls of Jericho fell after the people had marched around them for seven days"* (Heb. 11:30). Although their faith faltered in the past, at Jericho, the children of Israel believed and trusted God and His promises. Just as they were saved by faith, so we are today saved by faith (Rom. 5:1) Like the Israelites, our faith must be evidenced by obedience. The children of Israel had faith, they obeyed, and the walls of Jericho fell "by faith" after they were circled for seven straight days. Saving faith compels us to obey God (Matt. 7:24–29). We must build our house on Christ, the solid rock, so when the storms of life come, our faith does not fall and get washed away. *"Stand firm and you will win life"* (Lk. 21:19).

**Lesson #6: God keeps His promises.**

In addition, the story tells us that God keeps His promises (Josh. 6:2). He is the same yesterday, today, and forever. The walls of Jericho fell because God said they would and today God can knock down any wall that may be keeping you from Heaven, including *unbelief.*

Going way back in my memory when I was a 14-year-old seminarian, I remember an elderly Claretian brother (assistant to a priest) who was practicing self-sacrifice. He looked like Yoda with his sparse hair and tattered clothing. (Maybe the town in Spain where he was from was called Dagobah.) He refused to eat in the large lunchroom at a table with the rest of us. He found all his meals by going into the large trash dumpsters and ate food that someone had thrown away.

One evening near twilight I was walking past a dumpster, when he startled me by popping up. He looked at me and rhetorically said, "Wouldn't it be a shame if there is no Heaven?" He then chuckled in a nervous manner. I did not know how to respond, so I just said, "God bless you!" as I kept walking.

I've thought about this encounter at various times in my life. My conclusion (opinion) is in two parts:

1. This elderly brother was trying to earn his way into Heaven through self-sacrifice. All he had to do was believe Jesus's words, *"I am the Way, the Truth and the Life, no one comes to the Father except through Me"* (Jn. 14:6).

2. He voiced a form of unbelief when he said, "Wouldn't it be a shame if there is no Heaven?" At his age, he could have increased our faith by sitting with us and telling

us about his anticipation for Heaven. Unfortunately, he, perhaps, did not know how to.

Heaven is *real* and that is where believers will spend *eternity*.

God's promises to us today are just as certain, they are just as unwavering, they are exceedingly great and wonderfully precious. (Jn. 3:16)

God has done His Part by sending His Son to save us; now our part is to believe in His Son.

*It is so simple that only the foolish miss this promise.*

## Lesson #7: Faith without works is dead.

*"As the body without the spirit is dead, so faith without works is dead"* (Jm. 2:26). It is not enough to say, "I believe God" and then live in an ungodly manner. If we truly believe God, our utmost desire is to obey God. Our faith is demonstrated by actions. We must love the Lord with all our heart, soul, and mind, and we must love our neighbors as ourselves. We are blessed so we can be a blessing to others.

Joshua and the Israelites carried out the commands of God and conquered Jericho. God gave them victory over an enemy that was trying to keep them out of the Promised Land. So it is with us today: if we have true faith, we are obligated to obey God, and God will give us victory over the enemies that we face throughout life.

The walls of Jericho are symbolic for the barriers (things in life) that prevent us from living the purpose God has for each one of us. The main thing God wants from us is *to believe in His Son* and gain the right to live with Him in Heaven forever. That means all of us, even those who we might think are unworthy, yes, even the politician you dislike the most. God loves everyone the same and does not want anyone to perish. He is the God of second chances and still works miracles today.

Find your purpose in life and build the remainder of your life around it. Be a light shining in the darkness. Shine like the moon that lights up the sky at night (in the darkness of this world) The moon does not have any power of its own. Its light is a reflection of the Son. We must make sure others see the joy of the Lord illuminating from us in all circumstances.

## Exercising Wisdom

Scriptures show us how to live our life in the best and noblest manner. Some of my favorite scriptures on wisdom can found in the Old Testament in the books of Job, Psalms, Proverbs, and Ecclesiastes. In the New Testament, the letter of James might also be considered "wisdom literature" because of its approach to practical Christian living for us today. The bottom line is Christian wisdom means making fear of God the goal in life. *"The fear of the Lord is the beginning of knowledge, but fools despise wisdom and instruction"* (Prov. 1:7). This does not mean we are to be afraid of God like the boogeyman. It means we must be in awe of His goodness, power, and might.

We must demonstrate our faith in God by the way we live. *"For we are His workmanship, created in Christ Jesus for good works, which God prepared beforehand that we should walk in them"* (Ephes. 2:10).

Sometimes it seems like obedience puts us at a disadvantage when we see people who act ungodly getting ahead or having more material things than us. Remember, whatever the ungodly accumulate will remain on earth when they die. In the end we must hold on to our faith and we will see His Glory and our eternal reward. *"And we know that all things work together for the good to those who love God, to those who are called according to His purpose"* (Rom. 8:28). In the end, no matter what happens — *God wins and so do we!* Once we get to Heaven, *He will keep us safe forever!*

## Give Thanks in Advance — Look Way beyond Anything You Have Ever Imagined

Take a moment and go outside today — look up at the infinite sky with your arms wide open. Give God thanks in advance for that mansion in Heaven that Jesus made possible for us. Be full of gratitude because your name is written in the Lamb's Book of Life. One day we will be there with the great multitude along with the elders, angels, and four living creatures worshipping before the throne.

As you look up, feel your feet standing firmly on our earthly ground for now. Soon these same feet will be taking that first step into eternity — Alleluia! Demonstrate your faith by giving sincere thanks in advance. Raise your hands as high and wide as you can. Now bow your head in surrender to the Throne of the Lamb. Say the same words in John 7:11–12 that John heard from the multitude he saw in Heaven.

*Amen! Blessing and glory and wisdom,*
*Thanksgiving and honor and power and might,*
*Be to our God forever and ever.*
*Amen!*

It is powerful to feel in advance what this heavenly experience will be like. *Try it, you'll be blessed!* Being certain of God's promises and thanking Him in advance is a sincere expression of faith. Walk for the remainder of your earthly life in confidence because you have that same power that rose Jesus from the dead.

Remember, without faith, it is impossible to please God—You must believe! We just might be fortunate enough to experience the rapture before we die on earth. When will this happen? No one knows. *"The day of the Lord will come like a thief in the night. So then let us not sleep, as others do, but let us keep awake"* (1 Thess. 5:2,6).

How is the world going to end? Can anyone predict when it will happen? How bad will things get before Jesus comes back? From the coronavirus pandemic to natural disasters, many people are asking whether specific events are signs of the end times. The short answer is we don't know.

The real question, however, is this: *Are you ready for Christ's return?* You can be, by turning to Him and putting your faith and trust in Him. Commit your life without delay to Jesus Christ—the reward is eternal. Join me in our Golden Walk as we follow Jesus into Heaven. Until then, keep looking up!

*"He who testifies to these things says, 'Surely I am coming quickly.' Amen. Even so, come Lord Jesus! The grace of our Lord Jesus Christ be with all of you. Amen"* (Rev. 22: 20–21).

It is my prayer that Golden Walk has increased your love for our Savior and intensified your faith. Thank you, Jesus, because "You provide a broad path for my feet so that my ankles do not give way" (Ps. 18:37). I step forward with confidence and no fear knowing death, sin, illness, and every form of evil will be gone forever. When Jesus welcomes us into His Kingdom, there will be no more tears, no more pain, no more despair—only peace. The offer of eternal life through Jesus remains for us all.

*Will I see you there?* Until then—tell somebody about Jesus.

**Golden Step #17: By faith we follow Jesus into Heaven.**

J esus is in Heaven watching us during this earthly walk and prays that one day we ask Him to be our Savior. He wants to walk with us so we can follow Him into Heaven. The path to Heaven is narrow and lined with angels cheering us on to finish this walk called life. It is only through Jesus Christ that we will be able to eat at His table. Stay on course by walking with a narrow gait. Keep walking using the Word to be a lamp unto our feet. Life can be difficult, but Heaven is real, and there is no greater reward than the Kingdom of God.

God is watching us daily. When our walk is over, God will see us from a distance and give orders to "bring out the best robe and put it on, my child." His servants will be ready to place a ring on our hand, and the celebration meal prepared for you will be out of this world! We will be given a crown of life for walking in the manner of a child of the King. We will meet up with other saints to eat from the sweetest fruit ever grown...from The Tree of Life. Everyone will be praising the Lamb of God, the One and Only — Jesus the Christ!

Walk as if your life and the life of others depend on it because it does and they do. As believers we must do everything we can to help others follow Jesus into Heaven.

## Just Like Us with explanation

Just like Us
Little snowflake landing on the window
Displaying all of your uniqueness
Praising God with your one-of-a-kind features
Created by the Father
Just for a moment
Just like us

**Explanation**: I was sitting on the runway at Washington Dulles Airport. It was beginning to snow. A single snowflake landed on the window that I was able to examine closely. It reminded me how each of us is so uniquely made. God made us in His Image but different from everyone else. We are like snowflakes that are on earth just briefly.

Little Baby O learning to walk
Goodbye to crawling, so eager to talk
His whole life in front of him
Planned by the Father
Just for his lifetime
Just like us

**Explanation:** During a visit to Phoenix, we saw my great-nephew Horacio (nicknamed Baby O). It gave me joy to watch him attempting to take his first steps. Baby O was about to begin walking on his path of life.

Little Ariana sitting on my lap
Smiling hard even with a gap
Precious memory, Kodak moment
Created by the Father

Just for a picture
Just for us

**Explanation:** My goddaughter sat on my lap and smiled with a missing tooth. I had just told her, "Come on, Ariana, pretend like you like me." She said, "Aw, grandpa Tweet!" (in her squeaky little girl voice). Note: Ariana Lozano is now 16 years old and is a cancer survivor—praise God!

Ariana Lozano, my goddaughter.

Little frog stopping on the porch
Looking at the worm with hunger in your eyes
Then enjoying it for breakfast without giving thanks
Created by the Father
Just for a meal
Just like us

**Explanation:** Irma and I saw a long earthworm next to a bull-frog on our front porch. I tried to get the frog to move away from the worm as I wanted to use it as bait to go fishing. The frog held on to the wall as I pushed him. I went to look for a stick, and when I came back, the worm was "Gone-zales!" I thought about the frog not saying thanks prior to eating the worm. That's what we also do every once in a while, when we are super hungry.

Two little birds eating some seed
Happily sharing without any greed
Must be his wife, hopefully for life
Created by the Father
Just for each other
Just like us

**Explanation:** We love to watch the birds eat from the bird seeds we have provided for them. On this occasion one bird was sharing with another. We thought of us and other couples that are love birds.

Little leaf falling off the tree
Once full of life and happy as can be
Look at your colors
Brown, red, and yellow
Created by the Father
Just for a season
Just for us

**Explanation:** We love the vivid colors of fall as summer ends and coolness returns. Life is about seasons; Irma and I are now living our best days in the autumn of our life.

Delivering letters into each mailbox
Or cutting trees, or breaking rocks
Working hard to provide for at least forty years
Planned by the Father
Just for a lifetime
Just for us

**Explanation:** Shortly after my retirement from 39 years at the USPS, I reflected on how God provides careers to get us through life. I thought about our son Steve making a living at cutting trees. Whatever you do, work at it as you are trying to please God, not man.

Giving us life inside her womb
Teaching her children the right way to groom
Loving us always all of her life
Now living in her eternal reward
Planned by the Father
Just forever.
Just for us

**Explanation:** This last part of the poem was completed on December 17, 2015, at 1:15 a.m. I had just returned home from visiting my mother, who was terminally ill. This was one day after her 88th birthday. It was the last time I saw her alive as she went to Heaven on January 19, 2016. My heart was hurting, but I knew where she was going, and it made it easier to deal with her death.

This extra stanza is added to complete the poem and finish *Golden Walk: Following Wisdom into Heaven.*

For God so loved YOU
He gave YOU His Son
All YOU must do is believe
Just one choice — Right NOW
Just For Eternity
Just For YOU!

Do YOU acknowledge Jesus as your Lord and Savior?

## ABOUT THE AUTHOR

**R**uben Gonzales is a late blooming Christian author who uses scripture, life experiences, and humor to share his belief in Jesus with others. He is a Vietnam veteran who served on the USS Gray DE-1054. *Golden Walk* is his third book that completes what he calls the *Walking in Wisdom Series.*

He is proud of his "south of the tracks" upbringing in the barrios of Phoenix, Arizona. Opportunities in life have allowed him to live in twenty-four US cities. He has an MBA from the University of Colorado; his undergraduate is from Arizona State University. During 39 years with USPS, he held several postmaster positions and worked his way into the executive ranks.

He has settled down with his wife Irma near Austin, Texas, but looks forward to their next residence — Heaven.

See you in Heaven!

Follow him:
www.leomor820.com
rubengee820@gmail.com

# ENDNOTES

1 Lucado, Max, *In the Eye of the Storm* (1991).

2 Scientific American, "Do hippopotamuses actually have pink sweat?" (May 6, 2002).

3 www.inovaheart.org, "Fast facts about the heart."

4 https://teachmeanatomy.info — "The medulla oblongata."

5 www.everydaypower.com — Pablo Picasso *Quotes Art, Life and Greatness.*

6 www.vroomvroomvroom.com — *World's Largest Sundial.*

7 *Jewish Encyclopedia*, "Weights and measures" (1906).

8 Musixmatch.com, *Musixmatch App.*

9 Batterson, Mark, *The Circle Maker* (2011).

10 www.tyndale.com — "Lists of spiritual gifts and what they mean."

11 https://en.m.wikipedia.com — "Billy Graham."

12 https://endhomelessness.org — "The state of homelessness in America."

13 https://www.thoughtco.com — "A comprehensive list of generation names."

14 Meyer, Joyce, *Quote from Enjoying Everyday Life.*

15  *Seattlepi.com* – Billy Graham: *We're Sure to Recognize Each Other in Heaven* (2011)

16  https://en.m.wikipedia.com – "List of waterfalls by height."

17  https://en.m.wikipedia.com – "Christ the Redeemer (statue)."

18  Robinson, Charles, *Punching the Sun* (2016).

19  https://en.m.wikipedia.com – "New Jerusalem."

CPSIA information can be obtained
at www.ICGtesting.com
Printed in the USA
LVHW051650201021
700977LV00013B/401

9 781662 831522